The Halfway House

Also by Jean Winter and published by Ginninderra Press
Mindshadows

Jean Winter

The Halfway House

The Halfway House
ISBN 978 1 76109 047 9
Copyright © Jean Winter 2021
Cover painting: Jean Winter

First published 2021 by
Ginninderra Press
PO Box 3461 Port Adelaide 5015
www.ginninderrapress.com.au

To my sister Sandra
whose compassion and empathy saved my life

1

I was in a police cell sitting on a bench in a cage-like room, with bars between myself and the rest of the world. I reminded myself of a bird, with its wings cut. I was not alone, with a woman sitting opposite me. I did not want to look at her, to start a conversation, so I stared at the cement floor.

'What did you do?' she said.

I couldn't keep on ignoring her. I looked at her pink long hair and noticed she was very thin. 'I'm not sure,' I said. I remembered that I had done something terrible to my mother. *Did I kill her, hurt her in some way?*

'My name is Tilly.'

'I'm Gardenia.'

'You'll get out soon,' she said.

I wondered how she knew that. Her face was lined with wrinkles. She looked hard, rough and tough.

'See my arm. Look at the puncture marks,' she said.

I looked at her arm, the inside of the elbow. It was bruised and a blue colour with a gaping hole.

'If I keep on injecting, the doctor said they would have to amputate my arm.'

I felt sorry for her.

'At least in prison, I'll get help to stop the addiction.'

I wondered if she could get help. Prisons are known for their drug trafficking, or so I thought. I wondered what she had done, to be in this cell with me. Was she a dealer, or was she caught trafficking drugs?

'Aren't there other rehabilitation programs?' I said. 'Don't you have a doctor, a general practitioner, who will help?'

'No, I don't think a doctor will help, because I keep on using. Have you been in trouble before?'

'No, this is my first time in a prison cell, but I have been locked up before.' I didn't want to say that it was in a psychiatric hospital.

'You'll be all right,' she said.

It was not long before a policeman appeared, dressed in a blue and white uniform.

'Gardenia Baxter, you can see your lawyer now.'

'You're lucky, because I'll have to wait longer,' Tilly said.

I wondered why I was seen first.

The police officer unlocked the door. 'Come with me.'

I followed the officer down a hallway.

'Just wait here.' The officer pointed to a row of seats. 'You'll be seen soon.'

It was not long before the door opposite opened and a man came out. He was very well dressed, clothed in a dark suit with an ironed white shirt and tie. He had long blond hair to his shoulders. It was curly, not unlike a lion's mane. He did not have a receding hairline, a rare occurrence in men.

'Gardenia, come in.'

The room was small, with a desk and two chairs. I started to remember what had happened. I felt sick, I had hurt my mother. *I didn't physically hurt her, did I? I was angry, but it was verbal abuse, wasn't it? I know it's a case of domestic violence. Will I get bail? What is going to happen to me?*

'Hello, I'm George Watson, a free aid lawyer.'

Does that mean I don't have to pay him?

'Do you know why you're here?'

I tried to remember the past events. 'My mother said she couldn't put up with me any more. She was pleading me to stop, because I was angry, verbally abusive. I told her that it was my house just as well as hers. I had earned it, gardening, home maintenance, painting and repairing walls both inside and out. I said she should go into a nursing home. But she knows me, I really mean the opposite. I think it's because I'm scared. I really love my mother. My mother has helped me so much, when I had no one to turn to. I said if she doesn't want me around she can get stuffed. She doesn't understand.' I tried to remember just what did really happen and why I had been sent to prison.

'You did some property damage. Your mother wasn't sure how to help you.'

'She rang the police to help me,' I said. *So she called the cops. Just what I wanted, security again.*

'You didn't want to speak to her at the time,' he said.

I'm a weirdo, not to be trusted.

'Is there anywhere you can go, because you can't go back to your mother's home before you go into court.

'Have I been charged,' I said.

'We'll take one step at a time.'

I let this sink in. I was terrified. I had to find somewhere to live.

'Any family or friends you can stay with? You have a restraining order which means you can't go home for at least a fortnight.'

I knew some people, ex-patients I had befriended, but I thought it highly unlikely that they would want me. They had enough problems of their own. 'I could ask my psychiatrist, she might admit me, to stay in hospital for a while.'

'Okay where can I find her?'

Where did Dr Jarvie have her rooms? 'Kensington Clinic,' I said.

'I'll contact her and see what we can do. I won't be long.'

I was taken to the reception area. A grey monotone place, with a line of chairs sitting against the wall. I waited, ready for someone else to control my life. I sat in the foyer watching people come and go. Some were well dressed and I thought worked there, maybe detectives and others who wore uniforms. There were people who wore clothes that had holes or tears; they looked unkempt. I didn't want to generalise, putting them in a category, labelling those who didn't have money with a criminal nature.

The lawyer came back.

I looked at my watch. It had been forty-five minutes. I had to stay, do what was right. I felt too scared to do otherwise.

'Fortunately, I was able to contact Doctor Jarvie and she said she will admit you. You can go straight away and she said she would see you later tonight.'

If I can't go home, then how can I get my clothes? I have nothing to wear, no toiletries or anything. I will need to get my medication too. I had to have my Medicare number and my private insurance number. 'How will I get my clothes if I'm not allowed home,' I said.

'You can go home, but there needs to be a police presence. If you go now, I'll make sure a patrol car is near. Do you have anyone who can pick you up and take you home?'

'No, because my mother's the only friend I have. I'll have to go by bus.'

My anxiety at not understanding my illness coupled with the fact of the aggressive tendencies by doctors to try and dig into my brain to find the missing link, had in the end made my condition worse. I felt I had no control. I remembered Felixstowe, the public psychiatric hospital, where I was observed for six months. I didn't live in reality, I was told by many doctors, not smart enough to work out what was wrong with me. Their easy answer was that I was psychotic. In fact, I was in their reality and was in fear of them and the medication. I thought I would be institutionalised for the rest of my life. If I disagreed with them, told them they were wrong, they would think it a part of my illness and therefore their diagnosis of schizophrenia was right. I wanted to withdraw from people. I disliked them and was in fear of them. From my experience, they obviously disliked me, calling me delusional and saying my thoughts were sick.

I left the police station and made my way towards the main road where I would get a bus into the city and from there get another bus that would take me home. I didn't have the money to go by taxi.

I walked along the footpath as cars sped on their way to other destinations. The sounds of the passing traffic were loud and my senses were picking up every screech, the rumblings of vehicles on the bitumen surface. After twenty minutes, I saw a bus in the distance. I knew, even before I got on, that I would suffer a panic attack. They had been a constant part of my life.

I stepped on to the bus, pulling myself up with the aid of the handle. My movement was like a wobbly shuffle as I took hold of the rail. I knew the bus driver was concerned, that he knew I was mentally ill.

'Are you all right?' he said.

I nodded. I tried to ignore the rest of the passengers, I asked for the fare going to the city. Once given the ticket, I pushed it trembling into the box. The bus lurched forward and I held onto the pole trying to maintain my balance. I knew the other passengers were watching, aware of my disability. *They probably think I'm drunk.*

I found a seat and with trembling hands I put my ticket into my bag. I tightly gripped the bar in front of me as the bus moved on its way. *What has happened to me? I've been on buses before. I used to go out and enjoy myself. Now look what I have succumbed to. I'm a feeble idiot.*

I remembered the days when I would sit on the bus going to town, my first year at university. How proud I was. I was going to have a career and be somebody. *Perhaps I'm grieving for the past, a lost opportunity. Or was I so conceited that life had to teach me a lesson?*

I tried to calm my shaking hands but I couldn't stop my head moving like a rattle that was being shaken by a child. I felt like a piece of jelly on a plate. I visualised those plastic dogs that sit in the back windows of cars. They had ceramic bodies that were immobile, with heads shaking and jerking continuously.

I tried to stop the incessant trembling of my head. My teeth were chattering and the muscles around my mouth were stuck together hard like lockjaw. I felt like it was a terrible nightmare, a punishment from God and that it would never end. The bus jolted and swayed and I felt like I was flying in a cage, being tossed like in a scary ride at a show. The more I tried to control the situation, the more my fear heightened.

I tried to console myself, to eliminate the panic. *I'm just another passenger on a typical bus on an everyday journey going into town.*

I leapt forward with the bus pulling out of the kerb and I tried to follow the gears, moving me backwards and forwards, trying my best not to fall off the seat. I tried to focus my attention on the passing scenes. I saw regal homes with sandstone walls, some having cloisters and vast gardens. I watched the busy people and the tall grey buildings rising up to the sky. I tried to focus on the passing scenes of inner suburbs. I looked at the other people on the bus all determined to get somewhere.

I saw a man and he was staring at me. He had a long beard and his eyes were a piercing blue. *Is he going to follow me, is he a stalker? I'm not paranoid, but he can read my thoughts. He knows that I'm sick in the mind. I don't want anyone knowing that.*

I arrived home and saw a police car parked outside. I waved to them to tell them I knew they were there. I knocked on the door and my mother gave me a smile.

'I have to get some things,' I said.

I knew I had to be strong. I didn't want to cry, if I did, I wouldn't be able to do it, to leave my home and my mother. I quickly got my things together. I didn't speak to my mother and she never said a word. With my suitcase in hand, I walked to the main road to catch a bus to Kensington Clinic.

Kensington Clinic was still the same, a sandstone building with a bougainvillea climbing the columns out the front. I had been to Kensington Clinic before and felt frightened and safe at the same time. I thought the clinic was rather like a train where people would get on and off. I felt safe at the clinic, thinking I would get better there too. Doctor Jarvie was very kind to me and I liked her. She would usually change my medication and that gave me some hope. Trusting her was a big element in my ability to recover.

I noticed the coolness of the building as I entered. A nurse dressed in a white and blue outfit was in the office looking through papers. I looked at her, hoping to gain her attention.

'Can I help you?'

'My name is Gardenia Baxter. Dr Jarvie is going to admit me.'

'Yes, I was told you were coming. Doctor Jarvie will be in later to do the paperwork. You can go to the dining room and get yourself a drink, perhaps sit in the garden.'

'Thank you. Do I leave my suitcase here?'

'It's okay, I'll take your belongings. You're in room sixteen.'

There was a veranda in the garden with large wooden seats with cushions. There was an older woman sitting in the garden. I sat down near her but not so close as to invade her space. I stared at her wanting to say hello. I wanted to talk. This was a new feeling for me wanting to be social because usually I was withdrawn. I guessed that the woman was middle age, perhaps fifty. She wore a brown coat, a brown hat, and had brown hair. I wondered if she was hot. I was feeling the heat and I had a T-shirt and shorts on.

'Hello, how are you? My name is Mary.'

'I'm all right. My name is Gardenia.' *I know she wants something.*

'I had to come by taxi today. I have a car, you know, but somebody rammed into the back of me. I didn't stop short, like quickly, for that to happen, you know. They just weren't looking. I'll be picking it up, getting it fixed. It won't take long, the mechanic said. I'm just glad I have third party insurance. Who's your doctor?' she said.

I looked at her and I wanted to say shut up, can't you stop talking blah, blah, blah, who cares about your car? *Why do I want to know about you, or your life, if you're getting taxis or your car is a write-off?*

'What's wrong with you? Who's your doctor?' said Mary.

'Dr Jarvie is my psychiatrist and I have depression.' I didn't want to tell her I had schizophrenia, I didn't want to believe it myself.

'Yes, I know what it's like to be depressed. I come here every fortnight. I get maintenance ECT, which helps my depression.'

I remembered getting electroconvulsive therapy when I was in Felixstowe.

Everybody in a psychiatric clinic confesses depression as their real reason for being there. Either they don't know what's wrong with them, having little insight, or they won't tell anyone because they're scared of what psychosis means, or are just afraid of being judged by others.

'You'll get help here. Don't worry, everything will be fine,' Mary said.

I've heard those words before. If I admit that I have delusions and insight, then one can't really call me mad, can she?

A nurse came out. She was on the plump side and had dark hair. She looked Italian. 'Gardenia, your doctor is here.'

The nurse carried a board where she noted the whereabouts of the patients. I went in and waited near the interview rooms.

It was not long before I saw Doctor Jarvie leaving the office. She looked prim and proper, wearing a dress. There were tiny flower patterns on the dress material. She had a cream complexion and was wearing make-up, a pale pink lipstick, with a touch of rouge on her cheeks. She looked gentle and had a kind expression. She smiled and that took me by surprise. I needed to focus and remain calm because I wanted to appear rational. I had hopes of going home as soon as possible. I just had to wait for two weeks, until the restraining order had finished.

'Come in, Gardenia.'

In the interview room, the curtains were made of floral chintz. The two-seater sofa was made in a similar fabric. I saw flowers everywhere. Doctor Jarvie was slightly overweight but I thought that was understandable as her job was mainly performed sitting down.

I sat down opposite her and placed my hands on my lap. I felt awkward as if I was being auditioned for an acting part in a Charles Dickens saga. My character would be a poor peasant woman who had emotional problems because she couldn't get enough food to feed her children. She had to live in an institution and was trying her best not to fall into deep depression because of her circumstances.

'How have you been coping, Gardenia?'

Doctor Jarvie's face reminded me of my first Labrador puppy dog. She had soft skin and friendly dark eyes. She looked contented, happy and healthy. I wasn't scared of her, unlike the previous doctors I had seen. I didn't understand my behaviour, being angry at my mother and throwing the coffee table on the piano. *Mum was scared, so she rang the police. I can't go back home until I go to court.*

'I can admit you today, Gardenia, because I think your mother needs a rest.'

I felt offended that someone had to look after me, as if I couldn't look after myself. I was not a bad person. I tried to intellectualise it.

'I think it's the medication, Doctor Jarvie. That's why I was physically violent. The only thing that has happened recently was the change in medication. I think it's the Prozac. It irritates my mind. I have heard that Prozac can have disastrous side effects.'

Doctor Jarvie was looking at my file and was writing some notes. I didn't know what she was thinking or how she was interpreting my thoughts.

'I have all the symptoms of depression,' I said. 'I'm tired all the time, lethargic. I'm not interested in doing anything. I have no motivation or feelings of pleasure. My indecisiveness and procrastination make me less active. I feel overwhelmed by everything. I feel like a failure. I just make the depression worse. I ruminate all the time, thinking that I'm a bad person. I have problems doing everyday tasks and I try to change my thinking, but I can't. Making my bed and getting dressed in the morning is a major achievement.'

'Have I told you about the community house?' said Doctor Jarvie.

I shook my head.

'Your mother wants you to be independent.'

I can't think of leaving my mother, I need her emotionally and financially. I have to think in small steps. I want to be more active and enjoy life, to participate in the world. My ruminations, excessively thinking of my state was not going to make me better, so the idea of putting my mind on something else was in effect a good thing. If I take small steps, doing little things at a time, will give me a sense of achievement. I would be taking control of my life. Over time, my confidence will grow and my thoughts about being a failure will lesson. Just to try was a success in itself. I should trust my doctor. She's a nice woman. She has my best interests at heart. It might not be a bad place and I don't think it will be for long.

'I think it would be good for you. You'll have company and other people can help with shopping and cooking.'

I felt again the humiliation of having to be cared for and to be with other mental patients. I'm not mental, am I? How ironic. I want my mother to help me, and then I don't want to be helped. Being cared for by a system, that is something else again. I know I need help but relying on medication, to be controlled and dependent on chemicals, emphasises my insanity.

'It wouldn't be taking me forward, would it? I mean, I'd be losing my independence.' I felt embarrassed and ungrateful.

Am I too much for my mother? Would she rather have me somewhere else? She's getting older and can't do things like she used to. She needs some help now. Will I ever see her again? I help my mum at home, don't they understand that?

I remembered Felixstowe, where I was detained for six months. I eventually came home but I had to see the doctors once a week as an outpatient. I also had to have regular blood tests to check medication levels. They also wanted to keep an eye on my thoughts, my delusions. They would ask me the same questions over and over. How are your thoughts today, what are you thinking? I tried to talk of my physical universe, the way my body was reacting to being over-medicated. I saw the doctors at Felixstowe for seven years. I wasn't psychotic during that time; at least, I thought I wasn't. The doctors believed that the medication was working, keeping me stabilised. I believed being at home in a normalised environment made me better. I was scared of going back to Felixstowe. Doctor Jarvie had read my notes from there and believed, like the doctors at Felixstowe, that I had schizophrenia. I don't think she wanted to rock the boat and tell me that the previous doctors were wrong in their diagnosis.

Doctors tell me I'm insane. How can I ever think of myself as a good person and a good citizen when over and over you are told you're not like others? I'm weird, mentally sick in the mind. I just have to accept it.

Doctor Jarvie was looking at me intently. I wondered if she knew my mind and what I was thinking.

'I'm still having problems concentrating, with a poor memory.'

'That will get better. Have you noticed any change in your energy levels?'

'Yes, as a matter of fact, I don't feel like lying down so much.' I had used this withdrawal tactic before, to try and close my mind from thoughts I had not wanted to face. It had never been a successful therapy. 'I have heard from others that cognitive behavioural therapy is very good.'

'I realise that you've had to struggle, Gardenia, and finding the right medication is part of the recovery plan, but understanding yourself and the emotional triggers play a big part in CBT. Having awareness of what your thoughts are and how to deal with them and changing them can make a very big difference.'

'So my problems are related to how I think?'

'Yes, but chemicals can help ease that process.'

Doctor Jarvie's ideas were not frightening. It was a welcome change. I plucked up the courage to ask a question relating to negligent psychiatric treatment. 'The doctors at Felixstowe gave me the wrong medication. The effects of the medication have contributed to my illness or rather exacerbated it. Is that right?' I was amazed at my courage, to express such a controversial point.

'I believe you were over-medicated and, yes, I do believe that your emotional problems are partly to do with your past treatment. I also believe that considering your history with anxiety and depression it is best not to come off all the tablets but to reduce them.

So that is what is wrong with me, anxiety and depression. 'So you think if I came off all the tablets, I would get sick again.'

'Yes, I do.'

I was still unsure if this all made sense. I knew my paranoia towards the health system was not due to being psychotic. I knew that my anxiety was largely due to my fear of being locked up again. Was my illness related to changes in brain activity because of the medication, or was I actually suffering from a diagnosed illness? I needed to know the difference and I thought at this moment Doctor Jarvie did not have the answers and was playing it safe.

'My sleeplessness, anxiety and headaches are side effects of the medication. My wanting to eat all the time, my dry mouth and constipation are not the consequence of or symptoms of my illness then. My tremors, panic attacks, are side effects of all the tablets I've been on.'

'Yes, there are some drugs that can cause those effects.' Doctor Jarvie said it as a matter of fact.

I need a doctor to right the previous doctors' mistakes. I went in with anxiety issues and came out with post-traumatic stress disorder. It's all just a matter of opinion when it comes down to it. It's not about a label or diagnoses. It's just about treating symptoms. Using categories just makes communication easier.

I felt confused and uncertain, trying to understand a horrific health system. The Felixstowe doctors had jumped in with guns blazing, ready to diagnose me in one consultation. Their theories had turned my life into a living hell.

They've made a mistake and I've been misdiagnosed. I don't have schizophrenia. Although Doctor Jarvie doesn't believe that the sleep deprivation was the cause of my last psychosis, I'm sure she's hesitant to change the diagnosis of schizoaffective disorder. Doctors usually don't like to challenge each other.

'I'm afraid,' I said.

'What of, Gardenia?'

'I don't know. I think of myself.'

'I think it's more likely you have a mood disorder than a psychotic illness,' she said.

'Can you be psychotic even with very deep depression?' I asked.

'Yes, that is possible.'

'Can being over-medicated make you psychotic as well?' I was sure she knew what I was thinking: that my treatment at Felixstowe was bordering on abuse.

'Yes, medication and especially changing it quickly can make you very sick,' she said.

Well, it's all very well to say these things and imply that I don't have much wrong with me, but how do you get on with life after being told you're a worthless human being? On a disability pension and frightened you're going to be on medication for the rest of your life because you're basically insane? I feel like I have to continually change to meet the needs of society and their categories. I've lost seven years of my life and my former identity, whatever that was, has disappeared with it. Is it surprising that I'm in fear, having lost a crucial part of my being, my personality?

'So it's about understanding cause and effect, with cognitive behavioural therapy?' I said. 'Being aware of negative thought patterns and changing what's not helpful?'

'Yes, but not denigrating yourself either, but reinforcing a self-worth,' said Doctor Jarvie.

It's intellectual but practical at the same time. That does make sense.

I told Doctor Jarvie of my anxieties with falling over. 'I've been falling over. It's like having a blackout and it happens generally once a day.'

'And what are these episodes like?'

'I sort of jerk and then blackout and I feel my legs go underneath me. It's only for a second and I know when I'm falling, everything happens in slow motion.'

'Have you had these falls before?'

'Yes, a few years ago, when I was an outpatient at Felixstowe.'

'Do you know what they said?'

'I was having epileptic fits back then. I was taken off a tablet and then I was okay. My mother said they took the medication off the market. I also have a stuttering and stammering problem with my mouth and speech.' I wondered if she had noticed because, every now and then, I would have a jerking action with my mouth. It was an involuntary muscle movement, and I didn't know when it would happen but I was very self-conscious when it did.

'I think your medication needs to be changed. You need an anticonvulsant.'

'The shaking, it's like an epileptic fit, isn't it?' I said.

'Yes, but I think it would be a good idea to see a neurologist and have a brain scan too. I'll have the nurses make an appointment for you. While in hospital, I want you to think about the programme that's happening soon. It's only for a short period, to get you used to the community and being independent.

Will I really be independent if I need help from nurses and doctors and generally social services? Do I have the stigma, thinking those with disabilities were not worthy? The irony was not lost on me because I was judging myself too.

'I'll change the medication because I think the Serequal as well as the Prozac might be the cause of your anger.'

'I feel like I can't think on that medication.'

'Okay, I'll put you on Risperdal but only a small dose, and increase your antidepressant. You can have the Alprazolam PRN to help with your anxiety. I'll see you tomorrow night, and do think about this community house. One of the nurses will tell you all about it.' The doctor turned away from me and studied her notes on the desk.

I left the interview room and went to the formal lounge and sat down on the sofa. I felt for the first time a confidence that I could trust Doctor Jarvie. I looked at the caged fish in the large aquarium. At least they don't know of any other existence, only living in a glass aquarium. I felt sorry for them locked up in a small prison. I was devastated thinking I was a nuisance, an inconvenience and that I would be controlled by social services.

I'm mentally ill, stupid and brainless. I can't look after myself. I'm not going to be described like that. I have to agree, but does my mother want me to go? How can I leave her? My mother is my only support and confidante. The only one who truly understands me. I don't want to think of my mother dying. How will I cope then? In a community house, I'll get help with cooking, cleaning and budgeting. I must try to focus on the positive features it entails. Is it worth trying? Do I have a choice? Perhaps living with other mental patients might not be so bad.

I mulled over the aspects of living in a shared household with others who had a mental illness. It was not going to be fun, living with others who had major problems. I couldn't even help myself. I felt better in a more rational environment, at home with my mother, a place that made sense. *We're not all the same, are we, even if we have the same diagnosis?*

I was still young and so many people my age were working, pursuing a career. Purchasing a home, falling in love, being married were not events that were going to happen to me. The thought of not having a life of happiness made me close a door on my mind. If my journey was going to be so difficult, then it would be best to not even think. It was now my turn to push the lever to make my mind shut down. It would be my decision, not theirs.

I felt anxious and so went to the nurses' station to get my little blue pill, the Alprazolam. It relaxed my mind, or I thought it did.

Cordelia the nurse was in the glass cubicle, working out the medication and sorting through files, I assumed.

'Hello, Gardenia. I was told that you'e going to go to Pine View for a little while. It's a great place. You'll like it.' Cordelia left the office with the glass windows and came up to me with folders in her hand. 'I have a form for you to fill in. It's about helping you with your mental condition as well as social aspects and preventative measures.'

She looks like she has just discovered penicillin.

'It's important to have these details for the staff at Pine View and for you, so you don't relapse. They need some of these facts. If you find the form too difficult, you don't have to fill it all out, just try your best. You have plenty of time, no need to rush. When you've finished, could you please pass it back to me.'

I looked at Cordelia dumbfounded. *Did I agree already to this housing stuff? Oh God,, not more forms to fill in.*

The papers consisted of a detailed list of questions. The first subject related to personal identification: age, birthplace, current address, marital status, number of dependents. The next set of questions related to the patient's social history. Were they employed or looking for work, or on a pension? Did they receive community help or receive financial assistance from family or government? Did they live on their own or in a shared household? Details of education were to be noted and any hobbies or skills, interests. The next set of questions dealt with family members and their respective employment details and medical history. I also had to describe my significant physical health problems.

I looked at the list of questions and wondered if I was filling out a census form for the Bureau of Statistics. *That would be funny, wouldn't it? On Tuesday 9 November I was in a loony bin. Then they would have it on record.*

Other significant questions were asked. What are your goals? Where would you like to be in five years' time? The questionnaire was very extensive. The next set of questions dealt with my medical history in relation to psychiatry.

Do you have difficulties in concentrating?

Yes.

Do you suffer with anxiety?

Yes, I agree to that one.

Do you suffer with depression?

Definitely.

Have you been an inpatient in a psychiatric hospital?

Should I say no? They'll wonder about that answer. I'm in a hospital now. Yes, six months as an inpatient at Felixstowe public psychiatric facility. I didn't like it. I'm currently residing at Kensington Clinic.

What condition are you suffering from?

I haven't got a bloody clue or perhaps I should write schizoaffective disorder? I didn't want to admit the diagnosis. I have a generalised anxiety disorder, plus post-traumatic stress disorder. I know that's the case. I only have to think of my hospitalisation at Felixstowe.

The last section dealt with emergency contact details. Can you dream, set goals and have a happier life? Will you get support with motivation and have a mentor who will help you to gain insight into my illness and guide you? Can you be educated, participating with others who are going through similar situations?

I was trying to think positively, to brainwash my mind. Fake it till you make it.

After tea, I went to the nurses' station. I wanted to take another Alprazolam, because it helped ease my anxiety.

That night, I saw a nurse at my door shining a torch on my face. I wondered how they could tell if I was awake or not. I might have my eyes closed but I could still be awake. Do they hear deep breathing or snoring?

I dreamt of my mother. I saw her as a vision in my sleep. She was young again. I remembered her image from photos I had seen. I felt her presence. What did the dream mean? Was I being consoled by my mother? Was she okay and telling me I would be home soon?

2

The next day, I sat in the garden, trying to relax. I stared at the fountain of the girl holding the urn. I watched the water pulsing from the concrete vessel. I had no idea of its origins, who had made it and why. It was an ornament and I did not gain any pleasure from its construction.

I saw Mary again in the garden sitting under the veranda. She was in lighter clothing, a blue batwing-style kimono top and a long cotton maxi skirt.

'Does the ECT help? I've had it before and it didn't work.' The memory of frying bacon came readily to mind. I didn't want to go through that again, waking up seeing unconscious bodies surrounding me, like cadavers. It was like waking up in a morgue.

'It's really harmless, just a small intrusion,' Mary said. 'You're only under an anaesthetic for a couple of minutes.'

'I've heard it affects your short-term memory,' I said.

'It does but my depression is so bad, I'll try anything. Changing the conversation, are you going to the group today?' said Mary.

'What's it about?'

'Discharge planning. It's on in half an hour.'

That sounds interesting. I'll go to that.

When I was first admitted, I was given an introductory folder relating to the hospital's functioning. I thought it was just more paperwork, legal issues, forms about policy. I didn't want to read about detainment issues or the conditions of my confinement. I wasn't interested in knowing about the hospital's agenda. I had not realised it was information regarding programme schedules.

I found the room, after asking an obliging nurse. It was near the nurses' office and had a large sign on the door stating its purpose: 'Programme Room'.

I walked in and sat at the table. I wondered if I should have been equipped with a pen and notepaper. I didn't look at the other patients sitting, waiting.

A nurse entered the room, smiling broadly. She wore the same uniform as the rest of the staff. 'Hello, everyone, I'm Teresa, the programme coordinator. We're talking about discharge planning today.'

She stood at the end of the long oval table. She had dark hair and wore fashionable red glasses. I watched her flutter her eyelids. I had never seen someone blink so much before. I wondered if she had a nerve complaint. I thought she was stranger than the patients and that was a disturbing idea.

'Basically, discharge planning is about leaving the hospital,' she said.

She looked like she was interested in what she was saying. I wasn't sure if I was.

'Have any of you been to a group like this before?'

I looked at the other patients sitting around the table. I was surprised to see John there. I thought he would have been locked up long ago.

'I've been to this group before.'

'Yes, Guy, it's good that you're here,' Teresa said.

I had seen Guy before, the last time I was in Kensington Clinic. *I can remember some things. Am I getting better?*

'Me too,' said another woman who was sitting next to Guy.

I had not seen her before.

Mary was sitting next to John. A man was sitting in the corner. His head was bowed and I could hear him snoring.

'I've been in this hospital before, but I can't remember going to groups,' I said.

'Leaving the hospital is always a difficult thing, to adjust to the outside world and to govern your life. Making decisions can be stressful. That is why it helps to be organised. It makes life easier,' said Teresa.

I watched her flick her dark long fringe from her face.

'What happens if you don't want to go home.' said Guy.

There's always one.

'I think with the right help, it's imperative that you live in the community,' Teresa said. She was still trying to remove her hair from her face. 'If you're not well enough, then of course you should stay in hospital.'

'There are all sorts in the world, aren't there?' I said.

Everyone ignored me except for Teresa and she just stared at me through her long lank hair.

'What if it takes too much effort? What happens if you don't have the incentive or interest to want to go out in the community?' said Guy.

'I think then it's up to your doctor to make sure you are well enough,' said Teresa. 'This group is about making decisions when you are well enough to leave the hospital.'

'Perhaps I should leave, then,' said Guy. 'This group won't be any help to me.'

'It's okay to just listen and then you may find it easier when you do leave,' said Teresa.

I felt stressed just listening to their conversation. *Get to the point.*

'Is this about learning how to leave the hospital or are we just here for idle chit-chat?' I said.

'I think all our problems are important,' said the woman sitting next to Guy.

'There is a new programme. Just recently the hospital insurance companies and the government have outlined a new rehabilitation incentive scheme,' said Teresa.

Incentive scheme? You have to try and coerce patients to be rehabilitated? I suppose that makes sense if the programme is disgusting.

'The project involves helping individuals improve their social skills and challenge their anxieties. It's about community interaction.' Teresa had stopped blinking. Had she found a way to control her anxiety?

'You mean we get support when we leave the hospital?' said Guy.

'Yes,' said Teresa.

Guy sighed with relief.

How much is this going to cost?

'I want to reassure you that there are support systems out there,' said Teresa.

'Is this about Pine View?' I said.

'Yes, that's right.' Teresa had finally made a decision with her hair. She had found a large plastic paperclip in her folder and used it to push the strands back on her head.

A useful tool for a hairstyle. I must remember that.

'What's Pine View?' the woman asked. She had blonde hair and her make-up had been applied in a hurry, but I gave her marks for trying.

'It's a community house,' Teresa said.

'Like a halfway house,' the woman added.

'Yes, Joy. It's a live-in residence and qualified staff will help you with your problems.'

'How much is it going to cost?' I said.

'The government will use part of your pension to facilitate the scheme,' Teresa said.

'What happens if a person isn't on a pension or unemployment benefits or whatever? What happens if they're working? Do they have to pay for it then?' I said.

'The best answer I can give you regarding finances is that people who are working are usually well enough not to need accommodation such as this,' said Teresa.

'What you're saying is that we have to be mentally ill to be in a place like this,' I said.

'Yes, it's geared to those who have a mental illness,' Teresa said.

'Will it be like this place? Do we get our meals cooked and our beds made, that sort of thing?' said Guy.

'If we do, I wouldn't mind going,' said John.

The other man in the corner was still asleep.

'No, you'll have to do those things yourself. It's about being independent, but learning and receiving help at the same time,' said Teresa.

'What happens if you don't want to go?' I said.

'It isn't forced upon you,' said Teresa.

'What happens if you have no other place to go? Are you forced to go to Pine View? I said.

'Well, it would probably be in your best interests to have a roof over your head,' Teresa added.

It's common sense to me but I don't like the idea of being forced to do things.

'What happens if you prefer to be homeless?' I said.

'That is ultimately up to you, Gardenia,' Teresa said.

'That just says it all, doesn't it?' I said.

'What do you mean, Gardenia?'

'Do you want us to be poor and mentally ill so we can be involved in your rehabilitation scheme? If we don't go, then we're left out on the streets and then it's our decision to be poor and homeless.'

'I think, Gardenia, that you're getting confused.' Teresa's eyes were blinking again.

'Does social exclusion cause rehabilitation or is it the other way around?' I said.

'Okay, Gardenia, I think you're upset.'

'You can say that again. I'm not going to your Pine View home for the mentally disabled,' I said.

'That's up to you,' Teresa replied.

'I'll have to take these medications for the rest of my life, won't I?' said Joy.

I have started a revolution.

'We don't know the future, do we, Guy?' I said.

'My doctor is increasing my antidepressant. But he's scared because he thinks I could become manic,' Joy continued.

'I don't think he would be scared,' I said.

'You have to be relentless in trying to get better, don't you?' Joy said. 'Sometimes it's just too hard. That's why I come in here. I feel like I'm trying to climb Mount Everest.'

I didn't know what to feel. I was angry and ashamed at the same time. I hated being called mentally ill, but I felt sorry for Joy.

'I can't cope. I'm going,' I said.

'If you'll just sit in the dining room, perhaps make yourself a cup of coffee, I'll talk to you afterwards, okay, Gardenia.' Teresa was metaphorically holding out her hand.

'All right,' I said and I left the room.

I felt like a bad child at school who had to be sent out of the classroom. I also felt that I was on some kind of weird school camp and was adjusting to leaving home for the first time. Although my thoughts were disjointed and confusing, I had noticed a distinct difference in my mood. I wondered if it was my own thinking or the different environment that had caused the change. I wasn't sure if it was my trust and belief in the doctor's treatment, that new medication would solve my problems, which gave me hope. Like a placebo effect altering my thoughts, the 'power of positive thinking'.

I had the sense to recognise that my thinking could not be changed overnight. That it could only be the medication that had altered my disposition, to see life differently. I had learnt to live in the moment, but that had its adverse side. I knew that I had to agree to certain formalities of the hospital and treatment. I was first and foremost supposedly mentally ill. I could not disagree with this; my circumstances reinforced this fact. If I did challenge this idea, I knew I would be seen as irrational or paranoid. So it was a case of compromise.

I endeavoured in the next few days to tell Doctor Jarvie that my depression had lifted, but my anxiety had not diminished. It was not a lie, because it did describe my mind.

When I was due to be discharged, Doctor Jarvie asked me about my decision and my interest in Pine View and whether I wanted to live there. I felt I had no other option. Everyone wanted me to go. I relinquished my right to be free.

I saw my doctor again; she was dressed in a cornflower-blue dress with a pattern of tiny white daisies.

'Has the decrease in the tranquillisers made you feel better?' Doctor Jarvie wasn't interested in writing notes or looking at her papers. She was watching me.

I wanted to say honestly that I had no idea. I knew the importance of recovery and progression in mental illness. 'Yes, I feel a lot different.'

'I'm glad you want to go to Pine View. How are you feeling with the antidepressant? It's been nearly two weeks. Do you think they've had an impact?'

'I think so, because I feel a bit happier. I'm allowed to go to the shop on my own. I bought a book, about the grieving process.'

'I see.' The doctor looked in her folder.

I knew it was the end of the consultation.

'The medical doctor says you have high cholesterol and he wants to continue with some more tests because he thinks you might have diabetes.'

It's just what I needed to hear. It's like Murphy's Law isn't it, my life? A melodrama. Whatever will go wrong…

I didn't tell Doctor Jarvie I had been getting up in the middle of the night and going to the chocolate and chip automatic dispenser and gorging myself on the sugary delights. I didn't think she would see it as healthy. I knew the nursing staff kept watch and it was probably in my file.

'We'll keep an eye on that,' she said.

I visualised a pair of eyes sitting on my mouth.

'I think it would be a good idea to have you discharged at the end of the week. The nurses will give you details of Pine View, how to get there. Will somebody be picking you up?'

I nodded. I didn't want to tell her that I had no one except my mother and she couldn't drive. Actually, I was very grateful to be in a private hospital. It was the difference between survival and a slow, excruciating death. Felixstowe was an abattoir and you knew the outcome. It was a waiting room and it only led to one place – insanity.

After finishing the form, I made sure I had everything – my suitcase was packed and I was ready to leave. The nurses had checked my discharge notes, making sure the details were correct and relevant. The types of medication and their dosages all had to be stated and prescriptions filled as necessary. Papers needed to be signed because of the legal aspects to health care, as well as providing the necessary financial payments.

I didn't understand their policies and what I was signing. It all looked too complicated and I hoped it would be in my best interests. I thought about asking why all the forms were necessary, but I knew listening to health management practices would only increase my stress. The less I knew about hospitals the better.

I waited in the foyer of the hospital. The nurse was making last-minute adjustments to the medication, making sure of the dosages.

Cordelia gave me my medication in a brown paper bag. 'Something to tide you over, until you see the chemist and have your prescriptions filled,' she said.

I nodded.

'Is someone collecting you? Your family?' said Cordelia.

I shook my head.

'Are you going by taxi to the community house?'

I shook my head again. *Does she think I'm made of money? I have to go across the other side of town. A taxi would cost me a fortune. These people have no idea.*

'No, I'm going by train.' *Perhaps I should say I'm walking. Would I get a response. Maybe she might say – I live that way, can I give you a lift. I didn't bother to try and find out.*

'I hope everything goes well,' said Cordelia.

I walked through the automatic sliding doors carrying my suitcase. *Next stop, Mars. I felt like I was in another world.*

Kensington Clinic was on Albert Street overlooking the Fitzroy Gardens. I walked down this major roadway towards Macarthur Street. I would catch the bus into the city and then catch the train at Parliament House.

I was tired and decided to catch a taxi to the city. I could afford a taxi service just this once, but I was hesitant to use my money. I wanted to save the little I had. Cordelia had given me directions. Pine View was near Williamstown Road. If I caught the Werribee and Williamstown Line, it would take me to the suburb, Williamstown. The house was on the corner of Cockatoo Crescent and Williamstown Road.

When I arrived at the train station, I found the correct platform. I waited for the train that was to take me to another life.

The train arrived. I sat in a window seat and I watched the seemingly endless suburbs pass by. I saw small businesses, shops and all types of retail outlets, roadway petrol stations and blank brick buildings, a microcosm of concrete. Also I viewed a smattering of distinctive and ornate stylish homes, architecture from an earlier time. Now and then, I caught a glimpse of people sitting at the front of cafés and hotels talking. I wondered how they could be so at ease enjoying life. I envied their lifestyle.

Opposite me on the other side of the train I saw a woman who was applying make-up, fixing her hair and other things to make herself look adequate. I thought it was sad that she had to improve herself. That it was important to have an outer shell that was beautiful. Was she preening herself so she could attract a mate? Men only liked women who were good-looking. Nearly every fashion magazine I had seen always had a beautiful model adorning the cover. *What happens if you can't meet those kinds of standards? Those types of relationships are shallow, they don't last long.*

I had given up competing with other women to catch the right soul mate. I did not consider myself beautiful but I also had the added disadvantage of having an unstable mind. I felt like an old tattered ship made to sail the seas, but too fragile to cope with the rough gales and waves.

I saw an older man seated further up the train. He looked the opposite of all that was supposedly fashionable and admired in this age of beauty. He reminded me of the homeless derelict people living in the streets. He had on an old stained hat and a discoloured torn coat. He had a large woven carry bag by his side. I wondered if he had found his treasures inside a rubbish bin. He probably used tough garden gloves to dig his way through the remains.

The people collecting discarded remains reminded me of ants that were breaking down waste products. They were necessary, like vultures eating the remains of prey, to lessen disease. The homeless and the starving were energy efficient machines skirting the city streets, retrieving plastic or glass bottles, anything recyclable so they could obtain a very small amount of money. Perhaps it wasn't much but if they did that every day, what sort of earnings would they make? They weren't much different from second-hand dealers, only they weren't making a profit.

The old man might not have a roof over his head, or money. He scrounges daily to survive but is he happy? Would he like to be told he was psychotic, to take tablets for the rest of his life? Told if you don't take them, you will be locked up in a cell. I think I would rather be homeless. Perhaps that is why I see people talking to themselves on the street because what is the alternative? Living in a prison?

I remembered the guest house where my mother worked years ago. I was only eight years old when a man with a long beard came to the reception office one night. He said he was Jesus Christ and asked if he could have a room for the night. My mother told him she did not have any vacant beds but I knew she did. She told him to go to the Salvation Army down the street. I knew why of course, because he wasn't Jesus Christ, but then I wasn't sure. It was like the old Bible story with Joseph and Mary: there was no room at the inn. Although in this case he was mentally ill.

I looked out of the window again and could see people walking their dogs. I saw trees, mostly non-native, European birch, pine trees and other ornamental Asian fruit trees and hardy brush-type melaleucas that were on the side of the road, probably helping to negate car exhaust fumes. I felt like I was having some kind of out of body experience as if I was a moving machine with the capacity of thought. I was acutely aware of my surroundings yet I felt like I was numb. At times, I could feel my conscious mind evaporating and I wondered if I was going to pass out. If I did have an epileptic fit and have convulsions, what would other people do?

I liked to call my temporary home 'the halfway house'. It was a simpler definition and a better alternative to calling it a reintegration unit. Cordelia had told me it had functioned in the past as a medical centre and the rooms had been used by specialised doctors. It had been a successful practice, but was disbanded, because a larger and bigger medical centre had been established nearby. I wondered if the nearby residents appreciated its close proximity. The value of houses would probably decrease because of the community housing.

I heard the automated voice call from the speaker. The next stop was Williamstown beach. I got up ready to exit the train. I was nearly there. I walked to the end of the platform and looked around. Cordelia had said the street was right next to the train station. I looked over an expanse of brush scrub and saw the street sign, Cockatoo Crescent. It was on the other side of the tracks, but I could see a small walking bridge that joined the station.

I sat at the platform for a while taking in my surroundings, but I did look at the house on the corner. I was surprised and delighted to see a very large and beautiful building. Its facade was stone, probably built in the last century. It was like a manor, a huge building with ornate balustrades and balconies. The bluestone home was gorgeous and its luscious garden was spread around its perimeter. Tall gums and flowering natives were interspersed with darker shade-loving plants. On the other side of the street was a small park. I liked this sort of scenery – it gave me a sense of my English ancestry, the mother country, although I had never been there. *My God, I could live in something like this. So you're the halfway house. But you will never be my home.*

I felt alone, not in the physical sense but in my mind. As if I was not attached to anything. I could remember a time when I felt peace, but it was only a glimpse, a vague memory. Had I lost my identity and the only emotions left were fear and anger? I tried to formulate the psychological reasons for my fear. *If you are in fear, then someone or something has made you frightened.*

My only connection was with my recent past, the public mental health facility, Felixstowe, and its frightening conditions. *If I was judged insane and put with others who were also insane, isn't it likely that I would be angry? Wouldn't my opinion of myself be so low that I would be depressed?*

I picked up my case and walked over the bridge, towards a different future.

3

I picked up my case and walked over the bridge, towards the large two-storey building. I stood at the front gate and identified the number. Next to the front door I saw a sign. It read 'Pine View'. I felt apprehension. I wasn't excited with the thought of change or of my new prospects. Joy or happiness was an emotion that had been obliterated.

I knocked on the door and waited. I thought of turning round, catching the train back home. I visualised my mother opening the door, her smile radiating warmth, delighted to see me.

I glanced at the small shrubs and the bird bath and the rose vine that crawled around the columns. I looked at the cracked stone, black and white diamond tiling under my feet and a small spider in its web in the corner of the wire screen door. I could hear noise in the house and voices.

Perhaps I have the wrong house, perhaps I'm not meant to be here. I could go home, pretend this has never happened.

I heard a sharp cry and I turned to see a small miner bird looking at me. It was sitting on the stone path and then it hopped towards the nearby rosemary bush. *Is it a good portent to have something wild make a greeting, welcoming me to my new home?*

The door creaked and opened. The occupant cursed at it because it was jamming against its wooden frame.

'You'd think that they could make things better than this by now,' a tall man said, looking at me.

It's an old home. What do you expect? He doesn't look stark raving mad. He is nicely dressed with a white cotton shirt and blue pants.

He smiled at me, showing bright white teeth.

Obviously, he can afford to have regular dental appointments.

His black hair was combed flat against his head and parted on one side. His facial features were delicate and his brilliant blue eyes were startling. They were oddly light blue and clear. I wondered if he was an albino and had dyed his hair. I had seen him before and then I realised it was at Kensington Clinic. It was Guy.

'Oh, hello, I didn't know you were going to be here,' he said.

I smiled tentatively. Already I knew that living in proximity to Guy was not going to be easy.

'Oh well, you better come inside,' he said.

The hallway was dark and my eyes had to adjust to the different aspect, after being in the stark daylight. A collection of suitcases and boxes full of miscellaneous items had been placed just inside the front door. I placed my suitcase with the rest of the assorted items. The hallway entrance was carpeted with a long runner showing delicate details of red flowers. It reminded me of the William Morris designs of the twentieth century. I saw a hallway table and umbrellas standing in a tall cylindrical pot.

'Come in, then. We're just in here.'

I was led into a larger room. I looked around and studied the room. I did not make eye contact with the other people gathered. I stood by the door and looked out of the window. The curtains were white polyester with a sash forcing them back. This room was dark too, even though my eyes had adjusted to the light. I noticed a piano. Painting and pictures dotted the walls. It looked like a home that was well cared for.

'Come on, we won't bite. Just sit here, I'll get you a drink, you look hot.' Guy spoke in a manner not dissimilar to a very positive Avon lady.

'Yes, thank you. Water will be fine.'

Guy looked very confident and energetic.

He thinks he's in charge, I hope he isn't.

'I won't be long,' he said and raced into another room.

I sat on a comfortable large chair with patterned fabric upholstery, which also had a design of William Morris style flowers. Everything in the room looked like it came from the last century. The regency red and white striped wallpaper glared at me. I felt like I was in an expensive fluorescent prison. The floor was carpeted with a floral print and I wondered if I was living in an artificial flower shop. *Someone went to a lot of effort to decorate with this fashion of an earlier period, or did they get these items from a second-hand shop? I was expecting a maid and a butler to enter.*

I didn't want to look at the other people sitting near me. I had an odd sense of déjà vu. I had seen the clock on the wall before. It was a winding type and etched on the glass pane were a flock of geese flying. The bookcase standing adjacent to the clock was also a part of the odd feeling that I had been here before. I had seen the same books – the series of *Readers' Digest* magazines and a technical book on how to write and speak better. I had seen the large atlas before and even the spine that was ripped was familiar. *Have I been in this house before when I was younger or did I used to live here in another life? It was so real that I immediately thought I must be delusional.*

Guy came back with my glass of water. 'I'm going to live here too. Isn't that great? Have you met this pair yet?'

I shook my head. I looked at the older man sitting in the corner. He did not meet my eyes. I recognised him. It was John. I wanted to run from the house, never to return.

'This is John.'

Obviously Guy has a short memory, or isn't aware of past circumstances.

'Say hello, John.'

Guy is making introductions to a person I already know. He doesn't remember a thing.

'Hello,' said John.

'Come on, John, you can say more than that,' said Guy.

'I'll bloody well say what I like,' said John.

I thought the old man was about to get up and hit Guy.

'Okay, chap, settle down.'

I wondered if John remembered me. He looked the same, an old man, in his early sixties. His scruffy beard had bits of food clinging to it. He was wearing a stained T-shirt and discoloured pants. I wondered why he didn't care for himself or if he looked at himself in the mirror.

I looked at his feet, his thongs and his toenails and was astonished at their length. *An ancient Chinese emperor would be proud to have a set like them. He must be in pain. How can he walk?*

'Hello, I'm Gardenia,' I said.

John put his hand forward.

I wonder if I'm supposed to shake it, or does he want something to drink or should I kiss his hand? I shook his limp hand.

'That's better,' said Guy.

I'm living in Disney's Fantasia. *Guy is Mickey Mouse and John is Donald Duck.*

I looked at the woman sitting next to John on the sofa. I knew her as well and I was sure it was from Kensington Clinic.

'This is Joy,' said Guy.

I smiled and said, 'Hello.'

She was a big lady, broad-shouldered and top-heavy. She moved to pick up a glass of water from the coffee table. She looked hot and tired. I noticed that her hands were shaking. Her hair was lank and wet from perspiration. She was dressed in a soft, flowing Balinese-type sarong and turquoise blue cheesecloth shirt. Her clothes were wrinkled and torn in parts. I noticed her pink thongs and her toenails were short. *She looks bohemian. Perhaps it's a new avant-garde style.*

I looked at the patterned flowers on the chair upholstery. My head felt dizzy as I looked at the print. It was like an optical illusion. *I'm just seeing too many of the same flowers and it's making me claustrophobic.*

'I've got bipolar,' said Guy. He seemed to be proud of the fact. I was waiting for him to say, 'What have you got?'

I continued to look at the contents of the room. The paintings were in oils, most were of landscapes and a few of still life. There were framed landscape photos too. The paintings looked original, not prints. They were good and I looked to see the artists' name and date, but could not see any signatures. *Perhaps they are there but I need my glasses.* The photos were black and white, images of the Australian landscape – the outback, gum trees, small tin shacks.

It was an awkward situation, waiting with three people who were supposedly sick in the mind. To be involved with individuals who had a mental illness was not new, but the idea of living in the community with so-called sick people was unusual. I didn't know who was in charge or what next to do.

We sat there and waited for what felt like hours. I noticed we all looked at each other surreptitiously. I was sure it was because we had little in common or nothing to talk about. I hoped no one would bring up the subject of mental illness. I felt anxious and I wondered what the others were thinking. I didn't ask them and so I was none the wiser. *Probably just as well.*

The silence was deafening. Like a kind of impenetrable silence. To speak of my own inner turmoil was like recognising it as such. Perhaps we all had the same feelings. Not wanting to disclose how mad we were? I could see that we were all looking at each other and then quickly avoiding eye contact, pretending to be looking at something else.

I broke the distrustful silence and possible reflections on madness. 'Who's in charge?' I said.

'Sonia is. She was here earlier on,' said Guy

'She's coming back, isn't she?' the woman said.

'Yes, Joy, I don't think she would leave us alone like this, do you?' Guy said.

'I wouldn't know. I haven't been in one of these places before,' she said.

A woman entered the room. She was heavily built, wearing a blue uniform. 'Hello, everyone, how have you been getting on? Getting to know each other?' She had a Scottish accent. It was a thick abrupt voice but it also had a lyrical quality to it.

I wanted to get up and sing a traditional Scottish song, but then I couldn't remember any.

'You mean, have we introduced ourselves?' said Guy.

I felt a sense of relief knowing there would be some supervision.

The Scottish woman ignored the comment. 'I want to introduce you all to your new home. My name is Sonia.'

'We know that,' said John.

'Yeah, but she doesn't, does she?' said the woman in the torn Balinese dress, pointing at me.

I felt like I was being interviewed for a type of commercial franchise business or a pyramid-selling scheme. The Scottish woman looked like an excited real estate agent who had just won a commission. She placed some papers on the coffee table.

How does she know we are the right people here? We could have just come off the street?

I looked at John and Joy and their ripped clothing.

'I've just put the kettle on and hopefully the other staff will be here soon.' Sonia looked at her watch. 'Meanwhile, I'll pass out these folders and the information relating to this project. Please feel free to ask any questions.'

I felt like I had reached the heights of my career, I was a public servant in a boardroom, organising a new government initiative.

'I'll help you make sense out of all this,' Sonia said. 'It's straightforward but I know you're apprehensive – who wouldn't be – but there's nothing to worry about.'

I was puzzled and, looking at the others, I could see they were too.

'You can look at the information in your own time. No rush,' said Sonia. She left the room and could be heard talking.

I wondered if she was ill, talking to herself? I discarded that idea and thought that she must be on a mobile phone.

Who are we waiting for anyway? Aren't we supposed to be the mentally ill ones and disorganised? These people are in charge and they don't even arrive on time. Well, I'm in no hurry to go anywhere but still it's rude not to even show up.

I looked at John, hoping he was okay and that he wouldn't burn the house down or talk about evil devils and their purpose in this world. I tried to stay calm. My hostility would not make things any easier. I was trying to manage my emotions. I had learnt to block off from conversation, to ignore my surroundings, refusing to listen or take part. It was like a game whereby I would pretend that I was thinking of something very serious and therefore couldn't give any one else my full attention. It was necessary to try and control my thoughts in this way, before they became too confusing and overwhelming. I didn't want to go down a pathway, fall down a mudslide and then drown in a cascading river of brown liquid if I could help it.

Sonia came back into the room. 'I just want to talk generally about this project,' she said. 'This is a home firstly to help you adjust to living an independent life. Of course this won't be easy, but that's why we have set up homes like this across the city. We're fortunate to have this lovely home, so near the water too. I think you'll enjoy your stay here. I'll talk to you about the house and my position here and also what we expect of you. I am first and foremost the person who is running this home, so if you have any questions or issues, please see me. There will only be the four of you and you won't be sharing rooms.'

I sighed with relief.

'I'm expecting the other staff to be here soon. We have a maintenance person, Gustoff, and he also helps with the garden and cleans the home. There's Marilyn, who helps with the shopping and cooking, Josie, who is the program coordinator, and Greg is the other main supervisor. We all work as a team.'

I felt too afraid to move. I didn't want the others to notice my fear. I held on to my glass tightly, my hands were trembling. I was overwhelmed. Sonia had a lot of personality and I was not used to it. In fact, I was not used to any conversation, let alone understanding it. I had learnt to talk to doctors, and could easily talk to my mother, but with other people, strangers, I was hesitant.

'I think at this point, formal introductions are in order,' continued Sonia. 'Can you tell us your name and give us your story?'

Sonia looked at us and we looked at her. I knew this was going to happen and I was dreading it.

'Ladies first,' said Sonia, and she looked at Joy. 'Would you like to start, Joy.'

'Hello, everybody,' she said.

I watched her large frame rise from the chair. She struggled to hold on to the arm of the sofa as she prised herself up. She looked unbalanced and I wondered if she was going to fall. Sonia made steps towards her and then Joy righted herself.

'My name is Joy Black.'

Sonia smiled and nodded.

'I have had some problems at home and my doctor thought it would help me to be here. I would like to be more social, but I suffer with depression.' Joy sat down heavily back on her seat.

'That's good,' said Sonia. 'What about you, Gardenia, what is your story.'

'Hello, my name is Gardenia Baxter.' I decided to stay sitting down. 'I have a terminal illness and I need a break,' I said.

Sonia looked at me with a confused expression. 'Okay, well, let's hear your story,' and she turned towards John.

'My name is John Smith Rally and I have a few problems too.' He looked at Joy. 'I've been in Felixstowe and Kensington Clinic. My doctor thinks I could benefit from community housing.'

'That's great,' said Sonia. 'Last but not least,' she turned to the blue-eyed albino.

'My name is Guy Freeman and I have a bipolar disorder and some other things. My doctor wants me to be independent too, although I don't think I need to be. I can do things on my own but sometimes it isn't easy. I was finding it hard to pay the bills and that. Well, you know,' Guy said.

'Well, that's fantastic,' said Sonia. 'Now everyone knows each other, I'll talk to you about the home. There are four bedrooms upstairs, one on this level and that will be John's room.'

I looked at John's legs and then noticed a cane standing against the wall. I hadn't noticed his disability before. I wondered if he had been injured fighting in a war. *He did say he was in Vietnam. He might have post-traumatic stress disorder.*

'The bedrooms have beds, of course and dressing tables and wardrobes. If you want your own furniture, I'm afraid that isn't allowed. You can of course have smaller things in your room that you consider important.'

That means we won't be here for the rest of our lives. If I don't own my own wardrobe and some government department does, they will want more mental patients to go through these doors, if they are going to be cost-effective. I was starting to feel positive about my situation and even thinking Sonia had some good qualities.

'There's a bathroom upstairs and one downstairs and two separate toilets,' she continued.

'Thank God for that,' said Guy. 'It's horrible when you have to go and there isn't a vacancy, you know what I mean?'

I know what he means, but does he have to say it?

'All the rooms have all the necessities, excluding personal items,' said Sonia.

I wondered what she meant by having all the necessities. I wondered if toilet paper was a personal item.

'Our kitchen has a gas oven and gas stove top. It's well equipped with a fridge, microwave and pantry and also a water purifier. We have kitchen utensils, plates and cups et cetera. The fridge, freezer and oven are all in working order. The laundry has a washing machine.'

I wondered if I could work a microwave. I feared the radiation – we didn't have one at home.

'They give you breast cancer, don't they?' said Joy.

'Hardly,' said Guy. 'But then they do have them at your breast level, on the bench.' Guy looked at Joy's very large breasts.

'There's also a TV room and the TV set is available for everyone and there's a compact disc player and DVD,' said Sonia, ignoring the last comments.

'Have you got Foxtel?' Guy asked.

'No,' replied Sonia. 'We also have a therapy room which is suitable for group discussions and courses. Most of the management sessions will be conducted there. Greg and I will also be available at all hours as there's a staff bedroom on the ground floor as well. A large part of this house is blocked off for renovations. Are you okay about all this? Are there any questions?'

There was silence. I was sure Guy was going to say something about Sonia and Greg sharing a bed.

'Do you share a room with Greg?' said Guy.

'No, we have the same bedroom but I work for two days and then Greg works for two days and so on.'

'So you don't share a bedroom, then,' said Guy.

'No, not in the way you're thinking,' said Sonia. 'I understand that you all have different issues and problems and I hope we can rectify them. I know there will be pressures, coping with the inevitable problems that will occur. I want to give you hope that understanding each other, your shared fears, will make it easier for all of you. I will help you with your medication, education of your specific illness and specialised treatment. I'm a qualified psychiatric nurse. I hope this journey will make a new and better life for all of you.'

I felt like I had just heard a new presidential speech.

A person entered the house and I could hear them in the hallway. They were moving the suitcases and I could hear groaning.

'Hello, I'm here.' A young woman entered. 'I've just moved the cases and things to one side. They're in a dangerous spot. You don't want the health and safety people here, do you?' She smiled, showing a good set of brilliant white teeth.

I disliked her immediately. She was dressed too flamboyantly and was young and silly.

'Hi, I'm Marilyn.'

'Wow,' said Guy.

Oh, God, not another moron. I felt threatened by this young girl's easy-going manner. I was sure she didn't have a brain and, if she did, it wasn't working. Anyone who didn't suffer in life had to have a hide as thick as a brick.

We all stared at Marilyn. I noticed Guy looking at her breasts. I knew he was appraising her, just wanting her for sex. *Bastard.* Marilyn was attractive and very delicate, just what men liked.

These support workers are obviously not afraid of people with a mental illness, living together, in the community. But I'm certainly alarmed.

'Oh, hello, Marilyn,' Sonia said. 'This lady is part of the staff team and she helps prepare the food and other related duties.'

'You mean she cooks and goes shopping?' I said.

'Yes, that's right,' Marilyn said and smiled.

I don't think she understood my sarcasm. If she is naïve, it's highly likely she will have a horrible life. I wanted to tell her that there are sick people out there who will use and abuse her good nature. *Should I let her find that out for herself? Or on the other hand she could be highly astute with knowledge of psychology. After all, she has to know how to connect with the mentally insane.* I doubted the latter and so felt sorry for her.

Another man entered the room. His head was as smooth and bald as a billiard ball. *I guess he likes having no hair. I wonder if his hair was receding and he didn't like it. Maybe he had oodles of hair and just likes being bald.*

He also had earrings in both ears. On one side, I saw a sleeper and on the other ear he had a stud. I noticed he liked embellishing his facial features and saw a stud in his nose. I watched his nose twitch. I wondered if he had the sniffles. He reminded me of a rabbit. *Perhaps he has a cold or his nose is blocked.*

'Yes, well, here he is,' said Sonia.

The unknown and unnamed man smiled and waved. 'Hi.'

I couldn't help looking at his nose that continued to move. He wasn't using any tissues to unblock the congestion if there was any. I realised it was some sort of unconscious muscular reflex. *No one can move their nose that quickly. Does he realise his problem?*

'Yes, well. I'll introduce everyone again,' said Sonia.

'I don't want to go through all that again,' said Joy.

'Really, we all know who we are, don't we?' I said. 'We just don't know who he is.' I pointed at the bald-headed man. 'I'm sure if he works here he should know who we are.'

I heard the man who looked like an ex-bikie trying to make a vocal noise. 'I'm Greg.' It took him a minute of concerted effort to vocalise these two English words. He had a serious problem with stammering.

I saw Guy watching him in astonishment. The poor man, it was an unfortunate condition.

'Well, here we all are,' said Sonia. 'This is Joy, this is Guy and this is Gardenia. John is here with us too.' Sonia pointed to us respectively. 'You know Marilyn of course,' she continued.

'Yes. How are you all?' Greg said. Fortunately he was able to say this in a shorter time than his previous effort.

'Right then, very good,' said Sonia.

I recognised Sonia's surprise as she listened to Greg's short statement. *Obviously she doesn't know about his incapacity to speak. I sensed Sonia's anxiety.*

'It's always a bit daunting coming to a new home, isn't it? I'm glad that you all made the decision to be here today. We'll have a good time,' Greg said.

It took him much longer to say this statement. I was afraid that he would never finish, give up and walk out.

I looked at Greg and watched his nose twitch. It was quite large for his face, out of proportion. He had probably been teased at school and this reaction was the consequence, plus the stammering. *Or does he believe if he twitches it enough it will decrease in size?*

I remembered my bunny rabbits as a child. It was an interesting way of learning about sex, at a young age. Especially when I had to take the male bunny out of the cage when the female was giving birth as the male or buck would kill the babies. *Maybe that's why I dislike men.*

Greg was an unusual man, but then the population as a whole had many unusual people in it. It wasn't confined to people suffering with a psychiatric complaint. I had thought momentarily that the new male nurse might be my knight in shining armour. Instead, I thought his attributes were closely connected to my rabbit memories. Even so, it was comforting to think I had a pet bunny in the house.

'Before I show you to your rooms, I want to talk about emergency procedures,' said Sonia.

Oh no, not again, not more red buttons and traffic light dots.

'In an emergency, there are red buttons that can be pressed. They're all around the home. See here.' Sonia moved to the doorway and beside the light switch was a large red button.

'Fancy that being there,' I said.

'There's one in each room and one at the top of the stairs. They're all in the vicinity of the light switches,' continued Sonia.

I thought about the electrical system and how complex it must be. *This isn't a new home. Or are the alarms powered by batteries like the smoke alarm systems and just make a very loud ringing noise?* I wondered about John and buttons and fire and evil spirits.

'Perhaps we could have an alert system on ourselves,' I said. 'That way, if we're in any trouble, we could press a button on our chest and a great clap of noise would be heard for miles. Certainly we'd get attention then.'

I watched too many 'Prince Planet' cartoons as a child. Then I realised I remembered something I had not thought of for a long time. I wanted to tell everyone, but thought it would sound odd. I refrained from doing so.

Sonia looked at me and I could tell she was not amused.

'Also, there are more forms to fill out and to be signed related to privacy matters and freedom of information and your consent to have treatment,' said Sonia.

My consent to have treatment, I don't like that idea.

'I'll show you to your rooms now and you can make yourselves comfortable. When you've finished getting your things sorted, I'll give you a plan for today. We'll have lunch in half an hour in the kitchen. I'll talk to you individually during the day, to help you with any problems.'

I was the last to be shown my room. I carried my suitcase and followed Sonia up the stairs to a landing. There I could see, through a window, the garden at the back of the house. I was then taken further up the stairs to a short hallway. My bedroom was at the end. Sonia opened the door with a key and I entered the room.

The walls were covered in sickly green patterned wallpaper, with a flower print. There was a cane chair and wicker basket in the corner. A small desk was situated under the window on the other side. There was an iron-framed single bed with a floral patchwork bedspread. It was situated lengthways across one wall. The wardrobe stood on the other wall with a long mirror in the centre. The bedroom was clean and neat.

I went to the window and opened the wooden slat blinds. I could see the sunlight's reflection on the galvanised-iron roofs, the sparkling traffic lights and the steel poles. The light was so reflective it hurt my eyes like sharp flickering points that moved like light on disturbed pond water. I had an odd sense of feeling elated. *Everything is so bright. It's like I have lived most of my life in a dark cave. As if I have been living underground, travelling in tunnels.*

I looked at the phthalo-blue sky and the shimmering light on the trees. *Perhaps now I am at the surface, I can breathe some fresh air.*

I put my suitcase on the bed.

'Do you have your medication? I'll look after that now,' said Sonia.

I nodded. I opened the latch on my old brown suitcase and gave a brown paper bag to Sonia.

She opened itg and studied the contents in detail. 'You're taking Effexor, Risperdal and Alprazolam during the day and at night, Epilem. Is that all?'

I thought it was enough. The Effexor was an antidepressant, the Risperdal was a major tranquiliser or antipsychotic, the Alprazolam was for anxiety, and Epilem was a mood stabiliser. I had to remember what they were for. It kept me educated, to be in control.

Sonia looked at her watch. 'Good, I'll see you in fifteen minutes okay, downstairs for lunch. Take your time.' She closed the door gently behind her.

I inspected the desk, opening the small drawers. I found a pen and paper. The white sheets of stationery had the logo Banksia Mental Health Services printed at the top. I opened the wardrobe and saw that the hangers were not locked on to the rail.

I went downstairs for lunch. I looked at the kitchen, and the difference in décor furnishings and colour was dramatic. This part of the house had been renovated to modern standards. It was clinical with straight-edged lines and was stylish. I ate a sandwich that was prepared and then I excused myself. I didn't converse with the others and I did not want to look at the new house, the kitchen or its amenities. I went back to my room and stayed there for the rest of the day, hoping I would be left alone.

Later that night, I quietly ate my tea, a plate of salad and cold meat. I told Sonia I would be going to bed and she gave me my medication. I wanted to tell her that I was quite capable of looking after my own medication. I had done so for years but I thought it best not to influence or change her regulations, not just yet.

'I'm not supposed to give you these tablets this early, but as it's your first night, I'll bend the rules. I hope you sleep well, Gardenia. It's always difficult in a new home, with strangers, but don't worry, you're safe here. I'll see you in the morning,' she said.

'Should I lock my door from the inside?' It was a normal practice at Felixstowe. Intruders were a feature of the public hospital's sad atmosphere.

'No, I don't think that's necessary. I lock the front and back doors at the end of the day. Goodnight, Gardenia.'

I wondered if I should lock my door anyway. It had a lock on the inside and I was suspicious of the others. *Joy might steal my clothes. Although my two pairs of jeans would be far too small for her and my T-shirts would only go up as far as her forearm. Would I care anyway? After all, they're not designer suits but I can't afford to buy new clothes. I can't walk around naked.* I decided to lock the door. *They stole my clothes at Felixstowe, but I eventually got them back. If anyone stole my clothes here, I suppose Sonia would find them again, somewhere.*

I contemplated my existence as I looked at myself in the mirror. I had to change this situation. I wondered if these people could help me with my fears. If they offered encouragement and support, would my life change for the better?

Didn't they create this illness in the first place? They're the ones judging me as disabled or mad. I have to conform to their standards but how does that give me independence or freedom? They don't like me or who I really am, so they have to change me. Is it any wonder that I am depressed?

I will have to be aware of what I say. Make sure I don't disclose that I am depressed, sick, because then who knows what will happen? I can't stay in my room all the time, because they will think I'm psychotic, talking to myself. I won't make them think I'm happy either because then they will think I'm manic. If they know I'm thinking like this, then they will judge me as paranoid. Oh God, I'm confused. Perhaps they are right, I am sick, mentally deranged.

Doctor Jarvie believes my condition will improve. She's decreased the antipsychotic, therefore I will have a clearer mind, I won't be so sleepy. Even this new tablet, the Alprazolam, is making me feel a bit better. She knows I'm not schizophrenic, I'm not delusional. She knows I was only psychotic because I didn't sleep.

I tried to sleep, but I was sure I could hear someone screaming. I wondered if it was in my mind, or did it come from somewhere in the house? *Perhaps Guy is a heroin addict and needs a fix.*

I wanted it to be cold, where I could hear torrents of rain fall on an iron roof. I wanted to hear the strong winds tossing foliage, branches and leaves, to associate myself with something else that was also chaotic and turbulent. Most of all, I wanted to hibernate and to never wake again.

Sometimes I could remember my past, my childhood, and actually feel like I was there. The only reasoning I could find to understand such a phenomena was in relation to chemicals. I had recently been withdrawing from a very strong meditation, Prozac. I wasn't sure what it did; I think it was for anxiety and depression. My depression felt like a blanket that was covering my mind. I was unable to see the detail as well as the larger picture. My thoughts were jumbled. It was frightening removing that blanket to see a new world and having memories of my childhood. It felt like amnesia, and I was in recovery, remembering my earlier life.

That night, I had disturbing dreams. The images were quick defining moments, flashing scenes, pictures blending trying to tell a cohesive story. I saw myself lost in a dark forest, then an image of my face cut and bleeding. I saw a tree lying on the ground, its roots lying exposed, torn from the soil and Joy's dead body lying sprawled underneath.

4

When I woke, I felt by body shaking, like a vibrating battery toy. I knew that this physical trembling was not due to my own fear but the side effects of medication.

I heard a sharp rapping noise.

'Spud, is that you?' a voice said.

'Gardenia, time to get up, breakfast is ready.'

I recognised Sonia's voice but did she say 'Spud?' Her voice was sharp and I wondered if she had been there at my door for some time.

'Spud'? What was that about? A potato? I knew Sonia had not said it. It was a voice in my head, or a thought *Am I contemplating myself as a vegetable?* I visualised Sonia with a vegetable peeler scraping my brain, trying to utilise my mind for some productive purpose.

'Gardenia, can you hear me? Is everything okay?'

'Yes, I'll be down in a minute.'

I felt like I was Doctor Frankenstein's monster and that the psychiatrists were trying to change my brain, to make me a different person. They obviously believed my brain was degenerating. I wondered if there was a cemetery nearby. *Perhaps they're using dead bodies as test cases to change living brains? No, they're testing brains that are alive.*

I heard the chiming of the clock downstairs, ringing eight bells. I could smell the odour of disinfectant.

I pushed the sheet back and struggled to get out of bed. I opened the blinds and could see galvanised-iron rooftops like a patchwork of rusty panels, old, tired buildings, slowly decaying. I could see the esplanade and the electric light poles standing resolutely in concrete and the black outline of Norfolk Island pine trees in the distance. I understood why the home was called 'Pine View'.

I put on my light robe and looked at my reflection in the mirror and saw tree branches sticking out from my head. *No, that's my hair, isn't it? It's only my imagination, it's not a hallucination and it's symbolic. It's just my way of processing horror.*

I turned away and looked around at my oddly shaped rectangular bedroom. I felt the walls were slowly edging in and suffocating me. *Perhaps that's why Alice in Wonderland felt she grew so big and the room was so small: she was suffering from claustrophobia, or Lewis Carroll was.*

I didn't want to go downstairs, to face everyone. *I don't have to talk to them, do I? I can just come back to my bedroom. That way they can't form an opinion about my mental stability. They can't give me more tablets or send me back to Felixstowe. Sonia will be judging me, of course, but I just won't participate or get involved. I won't let them intimidate me.*

I went to the door, opened it and hurried down the stairs.

The kitchen looked like an antiseptic washroom, a cold informal place. It was the exact opposite to the reception room. There was a stainless steel basin for washing dishes, and a metal electric kettle and toaster were sitting on a white marbleised bench. The walls were white, the cupboards were white. The only colour contrast was Sonia's large body in a blue uniform, standing at the white wooden table, and a large noticeboard with a picture of a small Chihuahua dog grinning with false teeth.

The furniture and accessories had a functional purpose, without style. Everything was bland and neutral, without warmth. *It isn't really practical. You would have to be cleaning all the time to keep the place looking respectable. These people don't have any idea. My first complaint of the day and it probably won't be my last. Or have I been complaining all morning? I can't remember anything, but I do know where I am. This is a halfway house.*

I noticed an odd-looking stainless steel box on the kitchen bench. It was like a microwave oven but the dial looked like a lock on a bank safe; only the right consecutive numbers would release the door.

'Good morning, Gardenia. Did you sleep well?' Sonia's voice made an echoing sound in my ears.

Has she already said good morning?

'Yes,' I said.

I did not have a good night, waking at four a.m. and having to go up and down the stairs to find food. I did explore the pantry and the varieties of food on offer. Chocolate cookies in the biscuit tin were my first port of call. I assumed I would get back to sleep after such a good intake of sugar, but unfortunately I had to go back downstairs and find more appetising morsels. It was necessary so I could get a good night's rest. Next on the agenda was a large tub of yoghurt and a glass of milk followed by a bowl of strawberries. By the time I had ingested the lot, my sugar levels had outweighed my anxiety issues and I slept like a baby.

I looked at Sonia's badge on her shirt front displaying her name and 'Banksia Mental Health Care Team'. *I can remember her name. Does she think we are imbeciles? Probably necessary so she won't be mistaken for a mental patient.*

I remembered the psychiatric nurses wearing white uniforms at Felixstowe. I recalled the excursion, when patients and staff travelled to the city on a bus from the public hospital. We went to the cinema to watch an American comedy. The humiliation and embarrassment I felt with the curious stares from other travellers and passers-by. I felt ashamed at being singled out as mentally sick. Who wouldn't? *No wonder I'm paranoid.*

'I've read in your notes that you're on a new antidepressant. How are you going with that? Have you felt any difference?'

I could feel Sonia's eyes boring into me, reading my mind.

'Have you been feeling paranoid, Gardenia? I notice that you're very withdrawn. Are you still hearing voices? Do you know the difference between what is real and what is not?'

An existential question this early in the morning. My God, can she hear herself?

I looked down at my bare feet. I had forgotten to put my slippers on.

'Are you referring to my delusional thinking? I'm afraid, but I don't know why.'

I couldn't say I was frightened of Sonia and her judgement and this inspection of my mind. I was trying to see this situation as ordinary and that I was normal. *Does she expect me to be the life of the party, socialise, be friendly and enjoy myself, this early in the morning? Am I to be vivacious, happy, all the time?*

'Have you spoken to your mother? I thought you'd want to contact her.'

'I'm okay, it's just all new. I can't contact my mother because I'm under a restraining order. I slept well and I'm just a bit depressed.'

'Good. We'll have breakfast before you take your medication. Just cereal, I'm afraid, this morning.'

Is cereal frightening?

Sonia turned the electric jug on.

'I was expecting breakfast in bed, eggs, toast and a cup of tea.' I giggled at my own sarcasm.

Sonia looked around and eyed me suspiciously. 'What are you thinking about?' she said.

'Oh, just how pleasant it is here,' I lied.

'Really. I'd have thought you'd be uncomfortable at first, with the new surroundings.'

'Yes, well, it's a new start,' I said. I hoped such a general answer would stop the inquisition.

I looked out the kitchen window. I could see the next door house, its brick wall and a small patch of sky. Great view. I knew Sonia was staring at me.

'Bit of a grey day. Hope it doesn't rain but we need the rain, don't we?' said Sonia.

She's contradicting herself. She can't even make a decision about the weather. Its bloody summer, what does she expect? Why do people always have to talk about the weather? Surely there are more important things to talk about, like global warming?

'What are you going to do today, Gardenia? I thought we could have some activities to help us relax, get to know each other. It'll be fun, won't it? I hear you're a good artist, Gardenia.'

Yes, I am a very good artist. 'I like painting, I find it relaxing,' I said. *Joining the dots and colouring in, that's my speciality.*

'You'll have to do some here. I think we have some paints and things somewhere. I'll look for them, shall I?'

You can do what you like with your crayons. I didn't care if she turned the place upside down in her efforts to find some plasticine. I wondered why she tried so hard to be nice, but then she was receiving a pay packet.

Even if I do a drawing resembling a stick figure running in a splatter of liquid, she would probably say how much she liked it and comment on my talent. I could say I am going to exhibit it at the Royal London Art Academy.

I am a selfish, spoilt, horrible, nasty, sick, disturbed, hateful, undeserving shit of a person. I should be boiled alive in a vat of putrefied oil. At least I have the insight to realise my defects as an individual.

'How long do I have to stay here?'

'Well, that depends on the doctor and your health,' said Sonia.

I watched her looking in a cupboard. *I knew it. I'll never be able to leave.* I hummed the Eagles song, 'Hotel California'.

'If you can function independently, washing, cooking, life skills, then we'll think about you going home.' Sonia had finished looking in the cupboard and was now looking at the drain in the kitchen sink.

I can put my clothes in a machine. Does she think I'm incapable of putting cereal into a bowl? I'm dressed in pyjamas and dressing gown. I could sit at the breakfast table stark naked. Perhaps that's what they want me to do.

'Where are the others?' Sonia looked at the digital clock on the bench, the numerals displaying 9.10 a.m.

'Gee, time goes so fast when you're having fun,' I said. 'I mean, goes so slow when you're not well.'

'They should be down here by now,' said Sonia.

How would I know where they are? Maybe they have escaped in the middle of the night.

'Oh here's someone now,' said Sonia.

I wondered if I should shout for joy, clap and be amazed that someone was able to get up and walk down the stairs. *I am so nasty in the mornings, or am I always horrible? No, I am a good person. I must remember that.*

Joy entered the kitchen. She looked like a penguin shuffling along in her black and white dressing gown.

'Good morning, Joy. How did you sleep?' said Sonia.

'I didn't.'

'It's your first night here, it's strange for you,' said Sonia.

'No, I never sleep,' said Joy.

If she never slept, she would be dead or psychotic, although she does look like a woman who has never slept and she is by all accounts mad. Should I be thinking like this? Do people have thoughts?

Joy's hair was flattened on both sides and her hair in the middle was standing up like a Mohawk hairstyle.

'Hello, I'm Joy.' She looked at me.

'Pleased to meet you,' I said. *Weren't we introduced yesterday? She's just woken up. Of course she can't have forgotten the events of yesterday.*

There was another window in the kitchen that looked out onto the back garden.

Joy heaved herself from her chair and went to the window. She swept her fingers across the window sill, to test the accumulation of dust. 'Doesn't look like anyone looks after the garden,' she said.

My God, she's already complaining.

'At least we have a recycle bin.' Joy pointed to a large green plastic container.

I felt like throwing her in it.

'I like doing jigsaw puzzles,' Joy said. 'It sort of takes me away from myself. It's like the pieces are all unorganised and I can put them back in their right places. Then a beautiful picture appears, from a jumble of little mixed-up pieces. I think we'll get on great,' she said, smiling at me.

I heard heavy footsteps getting nearer. I felt like I was in a black and white horror film waiting for the monster to enter the room. Sonia and Joy were waiting for the ghoulish appearance. They looked like frightened cartoon figures waiting for the intruder to gobble them up. They reminded me of those M and M lollies on the television adverts, with little arms and legs.

Guy appeared at the doorway.

'If you sleep in like this, you won't sleep at night,' Sonia said.

'Sleep like this? I'm standing up, but yes I get your point. I don't sleep at night, that's why I've slept in,' he said.

'Your sleeping pattern should be regular and you need to wake up at the same time every day,' Sonia said.

'Okay, okay,' Guy said.

I was surprised to see his hair that had formerly been flattened to the side of his head had now turned into a dark mop of unruly curls. *Have I been hallucinating or does he use hair oil? Does he blow-dry it?*

He was going grey and he reminded me of an English sheepdog. He was wearing a black T-shirt with a printed image of a white bull terrier and the words 'all dogs go to heaven' was written below.

I was repulsed by him. I watched him stand in the middle of the room, his pyjama coat opened to reveal a chest without hair and a ballooning belly. I did not wish to look at his pants because I knew they would be the open-fly ones and I didn't want to get a shock. He moved his hand over his chin, feeling the knobbly and prickly hair.

I noticed Sonia looking at Guy. 'Oh, and by the way, there's no fraternising between members of the household. Okay?' she said.

Does she mean sexual encounters? I was alarmed at the thought. *Can Guy or John be a potential lover?*

Guy looked at me and winked. 'Later on, I'll come to your bedroom. Don't tell anyone,' Guy whispered to me. He put his finger to his lips.

My distaste was obvious. I felt like I had just tasted a rotting animal carcass and my facial expression signified it. *I am going to lock my door tonight. He thinks he is drop-dead gorgeous. He definitely has delusional problems or has an internalised identity conflict, because he looks horrible from the outside.*

'It's going to be bloody hot today. What's for breakfast?' he said.

I could no longer hear the conversation. It was like my brain had stopped working or my senses were temporarily out of order. I could hear mumbling, droning sounds and I could see shapes moving around me. Then there was a noise like someone scratching their fingernails down a blackboard. Then I heard distinct and understandable words.

'So are we going to do that then?' Sonia said.

What are we going to do?

'I'll have to sort out my room. My clothes are everywhere,' said Joy.

I visualised Joy's bras hanging form the ceiling light.

'Perhaps it's too hot today, what do you think?' said Sonia.

I felt like I was paralysed and only my eyes could function. Sonia placed a cereal bowl in front of me. I tried to move my mouth but I felt like I had been given an anaesthetic, a numbing agent a dentist would use. My gums were sliding back and forth as I tried to speak. I made a small croak-like noise. *I've turned into a frog?*

'You don't feel like eating?' said Sonia.

I shook my head.

'Not hungry?' continued Sonia.

I nodded.

'I think you should have your medication. You don't look well.' Sonia looked concerned.

I wondered if my facial features had contorted. I tried to think logically. *It's a reaction to the new medication.*

I saw Sonia's face, her big dark cow eyes looking at me with interest. I watched her go to the steel box that sat on the bench. She turned the dial saying the numbers out loud, 41632, and the door opened. She took out four plastic trays, similar to utensil organisers that hold cutlery. Each tray had a label – the person's name written in black pen stuck on with masking tape. Inside the trays were mixed assortments of various medications. She also took out a folder and looked at the notes. I reasoned that the papers described the appropriate medication for each member of the house.

Why do our tablets have to be locked up? Does she think I'll take too much antipsychotic? What was the number again?

I watched Sonia reading the relevant labels and reviewing the appropriate milligrams. She unscrewed a bottle and shook two blue tablets into a small plastic cup. She placed them on the table before me with a glass of water. I knew it was the Alprazolam, the anti-anxiety drug.

My arm was a heavy weight as I tried to move it. My endeavour to force my hands to coordinate with my brain was not easy. I poured the tablets into my palm and one by one I put them in my mouth. I wrapped my stiff fingers around the glass and then threw my head back in a quick jerk and swallowed the liquid and medication.

'There, that's better,' said Sonia.

I pushed myself up from the chair, steadied my body and walked hesitantly to the door. 'I'm going to bed,' I mumbled.

'I'll help you,' said Sonia.

'No thanks,' I replied. *I don't want a broken leg. You can't trust the medical system these days.*

'Don't be too long up there because you won't sleep tonight. We're doing some activities later this morning. I'll call you in a half an hour, okay?' said Sonia.

I kept walking and eventually reached my bedroom. I closed the door and lay on my bed pulling the doona over my entire body including my head. I lay there listening to my heart racing. *I'll be all right.* I repeated it over and over. Slowly I felt my muscles relax. I let go of my fear and slowly my mind drifted off and I was asleep.

I dreamt again of the forest. I felt little animals nibble at my skin. I saw my body decomposing. I tried to move but I was paralysed. I felt something soft and matted and I yelled for help and then realised I was touching my hair. *Or is it my puppy dog, Spot? I did have a dog, didn't I?* I felt her licking my face. I started crying. I felt a sense of peace as my canine friend continued to give me her affection.

Then I heard a picking noise. It sounded like an old typewriter. Then the knocking grew louder and I heard Sonia's voice.

'Are you going to come down? It would be good if you joined us.'

Why does she have to shout? 'Yes, okay,' I shouted back.

'Are you going to have a shower? Get dressed?' said Sonia.

'Yes, I won't be long.'

I fluffed out the doona and neatly spread the patchwork blanket over the bed. I looked through my suitcase and found the framed wedding photo of my mother and father. I placed it on the dressing table. I sat my Indian carved wooden box next to the portrait. Inside the box was a silver marquisette watch bracelet and a gold ring, my mother's jewellery. *Why do I still have them in my possession? They're only pieces of metal and sentimental rubbish. They can't help me now.*

I went to the bathroom and found a small piece of fabric hanging on to the shower tap. It was a mixture of colours and I refrained from using it. I had not thought of bathroom necessities. I had my toothbrush, toothpaste and deodorant. I looked through the cupboard and found a packet of soap, clean flannels and towels.

I looked at the small painting that was hanging next to the cabinet. It was a landscape, of a road in the middle narrowing into the distance with trees on either side. In the middle of the path there stood a man, a dark shadow, walking. The artist's signature spelt 'Vincent'. *Obviously it's not the original. Didn't he go mad and cut off his ear?* I didn't like the artist or his work. I didn't want to contemplate insanity. *Lovely. Someone must have thought a lot about putting that up there.*

I looked disappointingly at my reflection, the wrinkles and dark circles beneath my eyes. My head did not have branches attached to it but my hair looked like a red tuft of wiry mess. My eyes looked like clear marbles and the iris was big and black. I looked evil.

I wanted to do something with my hair. I didn't have enough money to afford a hairdresser. I brushed my hair, trying to control the curls and waves. I felt like a theatre make-up artist creating a hairstyle for a character in a play. I brushed my hair upward and it was so thick and dry it stood up on its own. I looked like the bride of Frankenstein.

I discovered an old red lipstick in the cabinet and wrote in large letters on the mirror, 'life sucks'.

I went outside and, as it was hot, I sat under the veranda, in a large wicker chair, next to Joy. I saw a very large man walk around the side gate. To say he was stocky would be an understatement. He had a rake and he made his way to the back of the yard. His baggy pants were stuck to the side of his legs and his checked shirt was waving in the wind. I watched him use the garden implement pushing the dried and dead leaf litter into a heap. His arms were pushing the rake, this way and that. My thought, at this particular moment, was his inability to use a rake.

A huge gust of wind picked up the leaves and spread them throughout the yard. I watched them spiral around in the air and then fall sporadically on to the ground. The man then left the rake standing against the side of the shed and began pruning the dead roses. I saw him go down on his knees and stretch out his arm holding the flowers out as if to an imaginary beau. Then I saw him pick up the rest of the dead flowers and put them into the recycle bin.

I looked at Joy and I wondered if she had noticed him. She was gazing at something far off somewhere else, perhaps in another world.

He had a big frame, red hair, beard and very large stomach. He reminded me of Henry VIII or some ominous colourful figure from the past, although his dress sense did not resemble a royal figure.

I need to get away from here. But where can I go? Even if I left for the day, I would still have to return. Didn't Shakespeare say that the world is a stage and that we are merely actors? Perhaps I can pretend I am someone else. I am sick of playing games. This isn't a stage and we aren't actors. I know Joy, John and Guy are sincere. They aren't pretending. Can they act, or recognise themselves as players on a stage? Can I win a part in this tragic satire of life? Would I bother to go to the audition?

I discovered that the meetings at teatime were a way for staff and housemates to air their problems, regarding practical matters of living in a shared household. It was a time to discuss new ideas and strategies, to make life easier. House rules were important and were to be obeyed.

We had a right to privacy and confidentiality but we were obliged to uphold a social morality, whatever that was.

Teatime was an appropriate time of day to have a meeting as mealtimes were an important facet of daily living. The likelihood of everyone being present was fairly certain. Sonia made it known to us that food was necessary and it was imperative that we should eat regularly, to remain stable and well. I had known this fact for some time but I didn't want to tell her so, to undermine her power. Jobs were hard to get in this day and age.

I sat in the programme room at six o'clock, waiting for the group to start. Joy came in and sat next to me. I moved to another chair as close proximity to Joy was making me irritable. Invasion of my own space, especially by someone who didn't use antiperspirant, intensified my frustration.

Everyone was there, including Greg, but John was missing. I was not surprised. I was sure he wasn't aware that time had a significant purpose in day-to-day living

Marilyn was neatly dressed, wearing a miniskirt, and her long black hair was pushed back by a white head band. She gave an impression of having a university education and that 'I know more about mental illness than you do'.

'Oh, hi everyone, I'm Marilyn. I help with the cooking and that sort of thing. I've already made some corned beef sandwiches and I've baked some Anzac cookies.'

The man who looked like Henry VIII, with a tank top on, exposing too much of his skin, was sitting next to Sonia.

'This is Gustoff. He's our maintenance man,' said Sonia.

'Hello, everyone.' He smiled and I saw his lack of teeth.

'I like your dress sense,' Guy said.

Greg was seated opposite Guy. 'I don't think that's appropriate, Guy. Let's be civil, okay,' said Greg.

Marilyn was sitting next to Joy and I was sitting near Gustoff and Sonia. I felt like I was participating in a conference with international delegates deciding on carbon reduction.

Perhaps I am about to watch a slideshow or am I in some weird cinema about to watch a documentary on how to take care of one's body? Joy could benefit from the programme.

'I am so glad that everyone has made it to this meeting,' Sonia said. 'First of all, I want to tell you that I won't be working for the next two days. Greg will be taking my place.'

I looked at Greg and noticed that his nose was still twitching.

'I want everyone to tell me how they're getting on and if you have any problems,' continued Sonia. 'You start first, Joy.'

'I don't have any problems,' she replied.

'Okay, what about you, Guy?'

'I don't have any problems either,' he said.

They are both delusional.

'Gardenia, how have you been coping?' said Sonia.

'To the best of my ability,' I said.

'Good. And John isn't here?'

No one replied.

'Okay, Gustoff, have you anything to offer?'

'No.'

'Good. I'll let Greg talk now about the agenda for the next two days.'

Greg was about to embark on climbing Mount Everest. He was going to speak. 'Well, I have a few plans for you for the next two days.'

I was amazed to hear him express himself without the least hesitation.

'I have some CBT theory to share with you all. Plus we can do some meditation. I would like us to go on morning walks. Do you have any ideas, anything you would like to do?'

'I want to go to the local library. Actually, I would prefer to go in the morning, as it will be hot tomorrow. Do you mind if I don't walk around the neighbourhood?' I said.

'I think it's in your best interests to attend. It helps with social interaction, and all the morning walks are compulsory,' said Sonia.

You're kidding.

'Do you know where the local library is, Gardenia?' Sonia continued.

'Yes, I've been looking at the brochures on the hallway table.' I felt like I was on vacation, living in a bed and breakfast hotel and discovering the sights of the local area.

'Good. What are you going to do, Joy?'

'I think I'll have a shower in a minute,' she replied.

'Okay, but what are you going to do tomorrow?' said Sonia.

'I don't know.'

'Perhaps you can think about it overnight. Guy, have you had any thoughts?' asked Sonia.

'Just a few,' he said.

'What are they?'

'I'm not sure yet, I'm just thinking about them.'

'Okay, we have all that settled. I'll pass it back to you, Greg.

'I don't have anything more to say, but I hope you all have a good night's sleep.'

I felt sorry for Greg, because his time on the block had disappeared due to Sonia's dominating presence.

'Oh, and before you go,' continued Greg. 'Medication will be at nine-thirty tonight and there's tuna mornay in the kitchen for tea. Have a good night and I'll see you tomorrow.'

I was relieved that the day was nearly over. I was going to have a shower after tea and then go to bed. After eating the tuna dish, which was quite good, I made my way to the bathroom. I had my nightdress. My toothbrush and toothpaste were still in the bathroom cabinet. I looked in the mirror. It was filthy and I could hardly see my face. The words 'you're ugly' were written on the reflective surface, with red lipstick. I took some tissue paper that was inside the vanity cupboard and wiped the red substance off the glass. *Who would write this? I had written 'life sucks' but who wrote 'you're ugly'? Was it John, Guy or Joy? Who owns red lipstick? It has to be Joy.*

I felt compelled to squeeze a pimple but I refrained, knowing if I started I would never stop. My face would become a huge hole and I would be forever eliminating toxic substances from my body.

I couldn't help thinking about mental illness and how I perceived myself in light of such an affliction. I also wondered how other people viewed me, especially those who lived in the vicinity of the halfway house. I had grown up to believe that people like me were strange and as such had to be locked up. The instability of the mind meant we were a danger to the community.

I could visualise the neighbours passing the house in a hushed silence only taking a sideways glance, before rushing on, hoping the illness was not infectious. *Do they think that the mentally ill are weird or dangerous, lurking behind closed doors, ready to pounce? Are they expecting to hear howls in the middle of the night or screams, imagining we are delusional and perhaps restrained in manacles? I could open the window and yell out, 'Help me.' I could rattle some chains and scream out, 'I've been taken prisoner' to the postman?*

I felt like I was strange or 'out of the ordinary'. I knew I was cut off from mainstream society. Institutions, isolation and barbaric treatments were common in the past, but it was still happening today in a different way. Exorcism was still being carried out, but under a different guise. I remembered a minister of the church visiting me after my discharge from Felixstowe Hospital. He anointed me with holy oil and prayed for my salvation and recovery. The church was my last vestige of hope as it was obvious to me that scientific problem solving had gone down the tube.

That night, I tried my best to relax and go to sleep. I counted the number of sheep that jumped over the fence, but I inevitably lost count and that made me upset, because I realised my memory was on vacation. I did what I usually did to counteract this anxiety. I went downstairs to see what comfort food I could digest. I wondered if Sonia was going to shine her torch on my face to see if I was asleep. To see if an animate living creature was there or not.

When I eventually did get to sleep, I dreamt of an old house and a man who was trying to fix a boiler. The heating system was archaic. I heard the water pipes groaning and reverberating as the man threw briquettes into the solid steel structure. Then I saw him beating the boiler with a hammer as if to stop the clanging of the pipes with brutal force.

Then the visions changed and I dreamt of a great big black pot, with three women sitting inside it. They had green hair and black glass eyes. They were in the process of being boiled alive. Then I saw the boiler man again; his face was disfigured with burn scars down his cheeks.

In the morning, I woke up in a sweat. I was shaking again. I felt my face and scalp for large boil-type lumps. It was going to be another hot day. I wondered what day it was.

I was putting on my jeans and T-shirt when I heard a strange noise. It was Guy singing in the shower. He was belting out, 'When you walk through a storm, keep your chin up high and don't be afraid of the dark…' Then there was a pause and he continued. 'At the end of the road is a golden sky and the sweet…' Then I heard him mumble a few words.

Probably forgotten them.

Then after a few moments I heard him continue.

'Silver song of a lark. Walk on through the wind, walk on through the rain though you're…' Again, I heard him mumble a few words and then he sang. 'Walk on, walk on.' Then more mumbles.

I felt like shouting out, 'with hope in your heart', as obviously he didn't know the rest of the song. *Perhaps he just can't sing that high.*

Then I heard him sing the same refrain. 'You'll never walk alone.' Then he made a humming sound.

If I can hear that down the other end of the passageway, then what are the neighbours hearing? The whole house probably needs double glazing.

Guy's singing sounded like a loud grumble of a train moving along its track. When he changed key, his voice sounded like the train had actually crashed and the emergency service was on its way.

At one point, I thought he was going to choke. *Perhaps he's training to be an opera singer.*

I had been told that the morning walk was to begin at ten o'clock, so I waited in the lounge room ready for the expedition. I saw Joy and her apparel. She was wearing a printed summer dress made from a synthetic material, which looked quite nice. She was also wearing dangly earrings and an imitation pearl necklace. I was impressed with her determination to look appropriate.

Then, what is normal these days? If she doesn't want to get dressed in a tank top and tights and wear joggers, that's okay.

She had brushed her thinning straight hair into some form of bun incorporating several hairpins, a rubber band and pink ribbon. She was also wearing a pair of heeled sandals and I gave her credit for her courage. They didn't look comfortable.

I had seen Guy and John earlier in the garden. They looked reasonable in their attire. John was distinctively dressed. His tartan shirt and striped pants were a mixture of pattern and colour. The odd colours, green, blue, black and pink, suggested he was either colour-blind, or enjoyed being noticed. Guy had decided to wear black jeans and white T-shirt.

I tried to remember all that I had previously been thinking, in order to understand my feelings. In my mental abyss, I forced my mind to evaluate the past. Clothes were a major subject. I looked at Joy and thought of jogging and then the idea of tartan earrings came to mind.

Greg had decided to arrive on time and we were all gathered in the lounge ready for our morning walk.

We walked out onto the street and down the path.

'This footpath isn't very good,' Joy said.

'This piece of bitumen was put down only months ago. The council is diligent about these things,' Greg continued.

We continued to walk along Williamstown Road.

I watched Joy hobbling on three-inch heels. *I know she's going to trip and fall over.*

Sonia said that it's likely my falling over was a result of many years of taking medication. It was like a Parkinsonian type of illness. She said that I just need my medication tweaked, to counteract the side effects. So I need a pill to help the side effect of the first tablet. I wondered if there would be a side effect of the second drug.

I was thinking about the side effects of medication, and trying to concentrate on Greg and what he was saying, and then thinking of Joy and her high heels. Well, this thinking led me down the road of seizures. My arms jerked in front of me, like a lunging effect. I felt my legs cave underneath me, and I fell. In slow motion, I watched the road getting nearer and nearer. I yelled.

'Gardenia has fallen over,' said Joy.

'I'm all right.' I got up, shaking and pressed my hands on my hip. I tried to massage the muscle, to help circulation. 'It's frightening and I don't know when it'll happen next,' I said.

'Are you okay, Gardenia?' Greg said.

I was beginning to cry, making short whimpering and whining noises.

'You'll see your doctor soon. I think he's coming tomorrow. We'll just have to be patient, okay. Put your mind onto other things,' Greg continued.

I nodded and kept on walking. *Putting my mind on to other things isn't going to help me. This is a physical manifestation.*

I found the walk tiring. It was not the physical exercise that had made me exhausted but my anxious mind. I was also upset at falling over and I looked at my feet with every step, scared it might happen again. I remembered the past when I was on medication that made it difficult to lift my feet from the ground. So if there was uneven ground, I would inevitably trip over. I also felt embarrassed, paranoid of being seen with unstable people. What I couldn't understand was why did I have to go? What was the benefit of participating in such an event? *Are they afraid of me getting lost, or do they think I'll walk out onto the road to deliberately kill myself?* I had no explanation, because I had caught a bus and train from Kensington Clinic to get here in the first place.

That night, I started to write down times, dates of events that had happened in my past. Not only did I want to keep track of the types of medication I had been given and the related reason, but far more importantly it would force me to use my memory. I knew that this was the most important factor in my illness. I could not track my thoughts, or make cohesive sense of my ideas. I could not concentrate and therefore I could not use logic. I was not trying to be smart to improve my employment prospects or to obtain a certificate. It was a survival tactic. If I could not rationalise, then my mind and life was lost.

I could not write for long, as my mind was closing down, due to the medication. I drifted unconsciously into another realm. Images and stories were acted out in my dreams, mirroring the events of the day. My doubts and fears were revisited and replayed like a jumbled jigsaw puzzle and I was trying to make the pieces fit.

5

It was an essential requirement for all the clients at Pine View to have a consultation with a psychiatrist. I was surprised that a community service with house visits was in practice. Sonia had mentioned that it was the government and private health insurance companies working together, but I was amazed that such a programme existed.

I was interested to know how my other housemates were to be treated, what their diagnosis was and the remedial actions to overcome their specific illness. I was interested to know the medication dosage and how the treating psychiatrist was going to relieve their distress. Such information could help me.

I heard a knock on the front door. I opened the door to see a tall dark man. I knew from my previous experiences that he was a medical specialist. He had the dignified air of being someone who could impart important knowledge. Plus Greg had told us at the previous meeting that the doctor was due to arrive. He was dressed in a light cotton grey suit and had a heavy black briefcase. His dark features were consistent with a person from an Indian background. His face was large and round and his bottom lip protruded excessively. I looked at his red flabby moist mouth and it reminded me of a swollen and infected boil. I looked at his dark eyes that were also projecting their presence. His facial features were essentially bulging and I was frightened. I wondered if he was a frog in a suit and he was going to jump on me.

'I'm Doctor Green,' he smiled.

I considered the idea of fleeing. Episodes of *Doctor Who* the television programme flickered through my mind. *Can I be involved in some fantastical plot and are malignant frog people going to take over the earth?*

He was early, at nine-thirty on a Tuesday morning, and I thought he was ambitious to think Guy, Joy or John would be ready – clothed, showered and finished breakfast.

'Please come in,' I said.

'This is a fine morning, is it not?' said the doctor. 'How are you today?'

'Do you want just an okay or a five-minute low-down, or a critical study of war and peace?' I said. I was getting used to his unusual appearance.

'No, crime and punishment will be fine,' he said.

That's an interesting answer.

'Please make yourself comfortable, there in the lounge. I'll tell the others.' I coerced the doctor to sit down on the colourful couch. 'Cup of tea first?' I said.

'No, I'm fine, but I would rather go into the study, if that's okay.'

'We don't have a study.'

'Then this will be fine, thank you.'

I watched him push away the paraphernalia of CDs, DVDs, paper and pens and other assorted items that were loosely confined between the cushions of the sofa. Other things, like lollies and old dried-up flannels, he left, possibly because of the probability of infection.

Flannels, how did they get there? I wondered how it was possible to have bathroom items in the living room.

'Who are you?' he asked. I had been asking that same question for some time now.

'My name is Gardenia Baxter. I have a doctor, Alice Jarvie.' I wanted to make that clear. I didn't want another interpretation of my 'mental illness'.

The doctor was quiet for a few moments as he was reading his notes.

He doesn't know anything about me. I have never seen him before. How can he help me?

'I hear you have been having some falls,' said Doctor Green.

'Yes, they happen spasmodically. I don't know when I'm next going to fall.'

'Tell me what happens.'

'Well, it's like I'm thinking of two things at once. I think to do something and my legs are going in that direction, but at the same time I quickly have another thought and my body can't deal with contradictions, so my legs give out.'

'Do you shake?' Doctor Green looked genuinely interested.

'Yes, I notice my hand and arm shaking.'

'Okay. I think we should run some tests and you should see a neurologist. He probably will want to makes some tests, an MRI and an EEG.'

'It's because of the medication, isn't it?' I said.

'Yes, it could have an effect, because you have been on medication for some years now. In the past, we used medication that had serious side effects. It might be the reason for your falls. Also, some of the medication you're on increases the probability of seizures. I'll write a script for Benztropine and see how that goes. The Benztropine is an anticonvulsant and can help with the Parkinsonism symptoms.'

Oh God, not more tablets.

'Do you like living here?' Doctor Green said.

'I think I'm safe here, because other people understand. But I don't know what'is wrong with me. I understand what anxiety and depression are but how can you control your thoughts if you're continually saying to yourself you can't cope. I know I have negative self-talk and I tell myself I'm not capable of living in the community. But I think these tablets are like a placebo. You think they help but in reality they're a sugar pill.'

His eyebrows were arched and had stayed in the same position for at least one minute.

The medication must do something. The chemicals are physical and the seizures are too.

I could see the doctor writing. I wanted to grab the paper from him and read his thesis.

'I don't like the past, doctor,' I said. I was thinking of Felixstowe. 'I never want to go back into the public mental health service.'

'I know, Gardenia, and we don't have to go back to the past. The future is all we want to see. This is a new beginning for you. I'll see you in a couple of days. Okay?' Doctor Green closed his file and took another folder out from his attaché case. 'I'm to see Joy Black. Is she here?'

'Yes.' I hurried off to find her.

Joy had been waiting in the kitchen. She had heard the knock on the door and was expecting the specialist. I thought that was the case by the way she was dressed. She was clothed in a new outfit, wearing a long viscose-type kimono part batwing floral top, with loose baggy pants. She had on a pair of dark sunglasses and she looked like a voluptuous Greta Garbo on one of her off days.

'Don't worry,' I said. 'It will all be over soon. Good luck.'

Joy made her way to the room where Doctor Green lay ready for the assault. Not long after, she came out, her interview over. 'John, the doctor wants to see you,' Joy yelled.

She came into the kitchen. She put the kettle on. 'God, I need a coffee.'

I watched her put five teaspoons of sugar in her coffee cup. 'How did you go, Joy?' I asked.

I had been eating the cookie biscuits that were in a container on the kitchen table. It was emotional comfort eating with the sugar giving me some solace.

'I told Dr Green that I've been very busy and didn't have time to speak to him.'

Joy was sitting with half her leg twisted behind the other leg and her arms were awkwardly draped around her waist. It was like they were looking for a place, a home where they could be comfortable, a haven for wearied appendages. *How did she get into that position?*

'I know I've been putting on weight. Doctors say I'm morbidly obese. I now have diabetes type two and high cholesterol. Now I think I might have heart disease and I've been told that it's related to the pills,' said Joy.

'Yes, there are some medications that can affect you like that. I understand why people eat junk food, because chocolates can increase serotonin levels. I don't know where I got that information, but it sounded logical.'

Doesn't serotonin help depression? It's hard even if you don't eat junk food and you exercise and diet, the weight just doesn't decrease.

'How did you go with the doctor?' Joy said.

'Okay. I told him about my falls. He said it might be due to the medication. I need to have some tests.'

'That's good. At least something is going to be done,' Joy said.

'I'm frightened that I'm suddenly going to have a seizure. I've been trying to break my fall with my hands, but what happens if I knock my head?'

I watched John limp into the lounge room to see the doctor. He was moving slowly and with great effort, using his cane as support.

If I can figure out their disorders, then perhaps I can find out what is wrong with me. I can obtain information. Trying to get answers from doctors is like pulling teeth – hard work.

John finished with the doctor and came into the kitchen.

'How did it go, John?' I said.

'I told the doctor that he could tell the bloody welfare department, I'm paying too much rent, for the bloody small room I've got and putting up with the others.'

I had not seen John so aggressive before, only psychotic at Kensington Clinic. *At least he feels comfortable enough to express his anger.*

'He's going to change my medication. I think I'm getting a stronger antidepressant. He wants me to think of something I would enjoy doing. He said to do a course or some form of diversion therapy. He said it would help me to be more independent and will reduce my anxiety and stress. He said he won't put me out into shark-infested waters.'

I was astounded by John's memory. How could he be so logical? I had trouble knowing what day it was.

'Doctor Green asked if I had thoughts about suicide. He knew I'd spent a lot of time in Felixstowe and wondered if I was happy here. He wanted to know if I had any goals or plans for the future,' said John.

I wondered what the doctor had written about John. *He has extreme apathy and unconcern for things and people around him. Not interested in communicating or being involved, perhaps depressed.*

I knew the doctor had a compassionate nature and I felt pleasure, humility and guilt at the same time. I also felt a sense of privilege that I was similar to John, Joy and Guy. I was grateful to have a mental illness, and this new idea was somewhat mystifying. I felt like a door had opened, just a little. A sliver of daylight had penetrated. I had a sense of being worthy.

'I forgot to tell Guy, the doctor wants to see him. Guy, the doctor wants to see you,' John shouted and it startled me.

I felt like I had jumped three metres in the air. *It's his home. He is allowed to scream if he wants to.*

I saw Guy running down the stairs.

'Doctor Green wants to see you. He's in the lounge,' said John.

'Okay then.'

There was a mirror in the hallway and Guy was looking at himself. He pouted his lips and turned his face from left to right.

Obviously he has delusions of grandeur. He thinks he's attractive.

'I think he wants to see you now!' John said.

'Right, okay then.' Guy didn't move. He was looking intently at a small lump on his face.

'Immediately,' John shouted.

Is John suffering some post-traumatic shock, because of the war, and was he a sergeant?

I saw John's contorted face and so did Guy because he scurried into the lounge room.

I sat under the veranda, on a wicker chair. The temperature must have been forty degrees centigrade. I thought about my dreams or goals. Perhaps write a book? Who would want to read my weirdo thoughts?

I visualised myself in Greece sitting at a table with a red and white checkered tablecloth. I could see the blue water of the Mediterranean and the sailing boats. I imagined a dark stranger sitting at my table.

'Would you like to join me for dinner?' he says.

Is romance possible for someone like me? I've been watching too many movies about middle-aged women finding love. Damsels in distress wanting to have a different life and expecting all their answers to be solved by a charming olive skinned, good-looking European.

I saw Joy in the garden sitting under the willow tree. *If there is a breeze, then sitting underneath the tree is a good idea.*

I saw Joy's three pairs of white large underpants hanging on the Hills hoist washing line. There were also about fifteen pairs of socks. Was a member of the house a caterpillar? Joy went to the line and took down her intimate apparel.

I saw a miner bird in the willow tree. It was native to Australia, with a grey body and black head. It had an orange-yellow beak with a distinctive yellow patch behind the eye. I wondered if it had made a nest and if so, Joy was in danger. They were an aggressive bird. My fears were realised when I saw it flying towards Joy like a dive bomber. It must have touched her hair, as I saw Joy wave her arms around although this didn't stop the bird's continued assault.

'It might peck out your eyes. Be careful,' I yelled. *I'm making her life harder and increasing her fears.*

Joy ran with her knickers to the safety of the veranda.

'It's only natural that it would defend its home, protect its children,' I said, trying to quell Joy's trauma.

'I don't care if it's Mother Teresa. I's a bloody nuisance.' Joy gave a deep sigh, and plonked herself on the seat next to me.

I saw twelve rainbow lorikeets sitting on the branches of the next-door neighbour's almond tree. I could see the miner bird had also noticed their presence and I was waiting to see his reaction. He flew at the parrots, darting around them, forcing them to move. The parrots that were twice his size ignored him. The lorikeets made a lot of screeching calls but were not bothered by his attempts to challenge territorial rights. They just jumped to another branch and continued to eat the almonds. Eventually the lorikeets flew off. I wondered if it was due to the miner bird's harassment, pleased to get away from his aggressive behaviour, or had they appeased their hunger. *I suppose they are not dissimilar to humans. We want homes with walls and fences, protection from alien forces.* I thought about how precarious their life must be. Existing day to day, making sure they had enough to eat. *Where is his water supply, especially in this heat? He has good survival tactics. The courage to take on a dozen parrots twice his size.*

I had noticed that all the house members seemed to be relatively sane. Joy appeared to have a logical thought process. I wondered what her problem was. I knew she suffered with depression but she didn't have any psychotic symptoms.

'What's wrong with you, Joy?' I said. After living with her for the last three days, I thought I had a right to know.

'I get upset easily,' she said.

Don't we all.

'Do you have a mood disorder?' I said.

She nodded.

'Do you accept what the doctors say?'

'Yes, I know I'm not well. I accept I have to take tablets but it doesn't mean I'm not a good person, it just means I have to make most of each day when I am well.'

'So you're well now?'

'Yes, there's nothing wrong with me at the moment.'

'What happens when you're not well?'

'I can hear voices and then my tablets are changed or increased and I go to hospital if I'm really bad.'

'Then when you're not hearing voices, you're just the same as everyone else?' I said.

'Yes, I'm normal.'

'How many times a year are you in hospital?'

'It depends, maybe four or five times. I stay for about two weeks, sometimes longer.'

'Then they let you go home?'

'Yes, when they think I'm okay.'

It was obvious to me that Joy's problem was a clear-cut case. She knew she heard voices. She took tablets to stop them and when she was well, she was just like everyone else.

Why am I under observation and why do I have to take tablets? What are my symptoms? Perhaps I am delusional, paranoid about doctors judging me. Do they want what's best for me? Are they saying I am psychotic and if so what symptoms do I have? I just know I'm sick, worthless. That's the real reason I'm here. I must be, if they have me on cartloads of medication. I can't ignore the fact that I'm mad. I've been in a mental hospital and they still see fit to give me tablets preventing me from being insane. Although Doctor Jarvie doesn't think I'm psychotic, at least I don't think so.

I know the medication helped my psychosis, but the hearing voices was related to sleep deprivation, not an organic illness. How can I test such a theory? Stopping medication could mean a possible psychosis. I don't want to be proved wrong, that the doctors were right with their diagnosis. It's a simple outcome for Joy. A chemical mix-up that has made her sick. But how can I have faith in doctors or in an illness I don't understand?

I noticed the geranium in the pot just outside the back door. My grandmother had said it was a good sign, as geraniums would not live where sickness was present. The plant looked healthy, so it debunked that myth. I saw that the potted herbs, oregano, sage and rosemary were barely alive. They were in dire need of moisture as their dry leaves were spindly. I found a bucket in the shed and went to the tank, filling it with water. I gently poured its contents on the wilting plants.

My life can be compared to the plant kingdom. I feel like a weed or a plant that's in the wrong place. Is it possible that I can be loved and not feel like a charity case or a piece of rotten food tossed into the compost bin? Am I slowly disintegrating and decomposing?

I felt like a fly caught in a spider's web, struggling for freedom. I was invisible, locked in a cocoon, trying to understand myself. I resented the fact that the medical system declared me mentally unfit to live in the community. They wanted to teach me skills so I could participate in society. I wanted to be tolerant, to be compassionate towards others, but I didn't understand why my life had to be like this. I hated humanity and I was angry. I felt guilty, having such animosity. I was confused and frightened

I watched the leaves on the willow tree move with the slight breeze. I saw the native bottlebrush, and particles of its red flowers had fallen to the ground. I thought of the idea of sustainable living. I could plant native shrubs and a deciduous vine on the northern side of the house. Perhaps passionfruit, which would stop the intense heat and give shade during the summer. Some hedging could be placed out the front on the south-west side, which would protect the house from strong sea breezes. I brainstormed other methods, like composting, mulching and placing plants in suitable spots. Saving water with a drip irrigation system and making a vegetable garden with companion planting. It would be a lot of work and I felt stressed thinking about it and by the enormity of it all. *Why would I want to go to those lengths, when it's not my home?*

I thought about walking to the harbour, sitting under a tree on the grass to watch seagulls fight over the remains of discarded edible rubbish.

I decided instead to have a shower. I went to my room and looked at myself again in the long mirror that was stuck to the wardrobe. I was not slim or good-looking. *Do I have charisma? I have a weird personality, but I'm honest and sincere. I do lie sometimes but I don't intentionally want to hurt others.*

I tried to brush my unruly curls into something that looked like a hairstyle. My hair was wavy, unconditioned and unmanageable. I pushed my hair back and looked at my large blue eyes, my pointed chin and the tiny freckles on my nose. I licked my lips and smiled, then turned away defeated.

I started thinking about symbolism and dreams. I would remember in the morning my night's terror, the disturbing images. Unfortunately my memory was good in that regard. I knew I had recurring dreams, a vivid technicolour world of creatures attacking humans and vice versa.

I looked out of the small bathroom window and could see the tall shrubbery – a tropical hibiscus tree with red vibrant flowers. I saw the noisy miner bird again; at least I thought it was the same one. He was sitting on the branch swaying to and fro with the light breeze. It made me think of the rollercoaster rides at the showground, people screaming, being tossed by the terrifying spinning machines. I felt like I was on a ride, travelling down a ravine and repeatedly falling over the edge of a waterfall.

The bird began to pick at its feathers, preening and cleaning its body. He had bright small eyes. I saw his little heart pumping beneath his feathers. He too had to face obstacles, hardship and trials.

I remembered asking my father before he died if he believed in a creator. He said he did. *But how can you believe in something you don't understand?* That was my dilemma and when I discussed it with him, he said, 'Believe in yourself.' *Ask a general question…*

I looked at the miner bird and I appreciated his courageous attempts to make a nest, produce a family and protect his young. The natural order was intrinsically good.

In order to believe in myself, I will have to find my own answers.

I tried to think of the positive things in my life, that I was alive, that I still had good physical health, relatively speaking and a roof over my head. Although the probability of a horrific event happening was likely, based on my own past hospital experiences. I couldn't imagine happiness. The sunlight and rain, all facets of daily living had a macabre feel.

I thought again of having dreams, perhaps travelling, having an overseas holiday. Then I thought of the movie *Mary Poppins* and the bird woman sitting on the steps of the bank calling out for donations, begging, so she could feed the birds. Would seeing poverty in another part of the world make me feel better? I couldn't change things, not now – I had to face my circumstances.

Life at the halfway house was not dictated by routine or order, although an aspect of minimal organisation was necessary for a well functioning household. I was allowed some freedom and therefore I was partly in control of my circumstances. However, participating in activities like the therapy groups were compulsory. I did respect that it was important, especially if it helped.

I could use my time in any way I wished, although some rules and regulations needed to be adhered to, like health and safety issues. Regular mealtimes and a healthy diet and physical exercise were recommended, as was taking medication.

I stood at the kitchen sink and thought about Sonia's ideas on behavioural change. The programmes she wanted to initiate, social activities and life skills like meal planning and preparation. *She obviously believes that productivity is a necessary part of recovery.*

The groups were about managing a mental illness and living comfortably in the community. Sonia explained that it was a difficult process. That psychological restructuring was hard work, and open and honest communication was essential. The recovery process was about identifying unhelpful thoughts and emotions. Lack of motivation, procrastination and avoidance continued a negative vicious cycle. Encouragement and praise, celebrating achievements and respecting persistence were important factors in overcoming and mastering difficult problems. It was a case of making realistic and flexible decisions and having clarity of mind that was not self-defeating.

That night when I was in bed I heard strange noises coming from the walls in my bedroom. Loud picking sounds that changed in volume, diminishing into silence and then returning again. I wondered if there were possums in the roof. It was an irritating noise, with the unrelenting, frustrating knocks. I would bang the wall in frustration, but the pick, pick, picking went on. I thought it was probably some small animal, maybe a rat.

I thought about the last three days. I had been taken on a tour of the suburb, fallen over, seen a frog-like doctor and coped with the other clients. I learnt to question my sanity because I was obviously unhinged. A miner bird was attacking the occupants of the halfway house, like the

Hitchcock film *The Birds*. I was also scared of walking, because I might have a seizure.

The medication had made its final assault for the day and I went into the darker realms of the unconscious mind. My last thought as I quickly fell into lullaby land was about the tenacity and courage of a small miner bird.

6

The next morning, I managed to eat a bowl of cereal, have a shower and say some pleasantries to the other occupants without any catastrophic events occurring. I heard the postman drive down the street on his motorbike but I didn't venture to look in the letter box. When my curiosity outweighed my nonchalance, I inevitably found letters addressed to the staff but this was seldom. Junk mail was prolific and Joy found such advertising material enlightening. It nourished her increasing appetite for products related to interior decorating.

Joy was an untidy person who had an ability to leave a trail of mess behind her. I was the opposite with an obsession for cleanliness, orderliness and germ warfare in general. I wanted things organised and my attempts to experience such a quality of life was an impossible dream. I had to reconcile myself with the chaos surrounding me – the discoloured coffee cups that were never cleaned properly, the waste bin that was always overflowing, the lolly and chip packets that were left lying on various horizontal surfaces.

I would not have minded so much except I had an eye for detail. Finding squashed sticky bits of food on my skin was always an unexpected surprise. The stairway rails, light switches, door knobs, cupboard handles and other miscellaneous places were surface areas I could not avoid. Therefore, having something moist and foreign under my hands often occurred.

I knew John had engineered this fiendish plot. He was having a horrible life and revenge was an understandable motive. He wanted to make life miserable for others and he was succeeding. My frustration would creep up on me like a semi-trailer wanting to pass a Mini on an outback road.

I think my possible obsessive compulsive disorder was appreciated by the other members of the household. I disapproved of such unhygienic habits and attempted to discuss the matter. My forceful opinion was heard because I knew that ignorance in such matters could only lead to death and devastation. Diseases, bacteria, infections, viral bodies that lived within the house had to be addressed. Unfortunately, my audience was not interested or concerned with my views. This did not vanquish my desire to impart information and logical reasoning was my ammunition. The arguments that resulted from my endeavours to divulge important knowledge reinforced my theories. The people I lived with were irrational and stupid.

I tried to excuse their behaviour and make allowances for them. We were having a heatwave and in such circumstances, rage, losing one's temper is normal. Our communal frustration and disregard for each other was best exemplified at the teatime meetings. I think I helped the other members of the household to express their feelings and emotions.

Sonia was organising another course: stress management. She said it was about cognitive restructuring, understanding irrational core beliefs and learning techniques to avoid and control anxiety. She pinned the details of the forthcoming course on the noticeboard. She also placed another notice on the board, outlining 'Basic Human Rights'. It listed several points referring to learned behaviour.

1. Flexibility, what is it?
2. Self-responsibility, what is it?
3. The right to challenge.
4. Perspective: am I mind reading or fortune telling? Am I labelling or overgeneralising? Do I have black and white thinking?
5. Making rules, but not saying I should or I must.
6. The right to be ill.

I wondered if this last point was necessary and also its relevance to 'basic human rights'.

Underneath this notice was another version of 'Basic Human

Rights'. I could tell that Guy had written this alternative, not only from his handwriting but by the subject matter.

1. The right not to be told you're a lunatic.
2. The right not to be burnt at the stake.
3. The right not to be burnt at all.
4. The right not to have demons exorcised from your person.
5. The right not to be canonised as a saint, just because...
   A. you saw a vision of the Virgin Mary.
   B. you saw a vision of the Virgin Mary and Jesus.
   C. you were told by a complex thought process what the meaning of life was and then forgot it.
   D. you performed three miracles such as
      1. cured obesity by not eating.
      2. had a good night's sleep without taking medication.
      3. laughed a lot even though diagnosed with depression.
      4. told you were mad because you had depression and then felt happy. (This was closely linked to the previous point.)
   5. The right to feel the bloody way I want to.

I found Sonia in the lounge room. She was picking up the empty crisp packets and other miscellaneous items.

'I want to ask you a few questions,' I said. 'The doctor thinks my seizures could be because of my medication. He is not exactly saying it is, but he wants me to have some tests.'

'Yes, I know,' said Sonia.

'What's an MRI?'

'It stands for magnetic resonance imaging. It's a test that uses powerful magnetic and radio frequency pulses to obtain high-resolution images of the body. It can be used to see body parts such as bones, muscles, ligaments, nerves, spine, heart, pelvic organs and in your case, the brain.'

'What's an EEG?' I asked.

'That's an electroencephalogram,' said Sonia.

That's a mouthful.

'It's used to measure the electrical activity of the brain. A number of electrodes are applied to the scalp. An EEG can help diagnose a number of conditions including epilepsy, sleep disorders and brain tumours.'

I was starting to get scared.

'The procedure is painless and you don't have to shave your head, but you need to wash your hair afterwards to remove the gel. The results will be sent to your neurologist and in turn to your psychiatrist and general practitioner.'

I tried not to think of the worst, that I might have a brain tumour, but it was a good idea to get a test. Ultimately, it would help me.

Sonia organised the appointment time for the next day. She said that I could have a travel voucher to get to the Royal Melbourne hospital. I was grateful to get help with my anxiety, travelling on buses. I was scared of having a panic attack again. My insecurities had increased with the probability of having seizures.

A therapy class was to take place in the programme room. Sonia was leading the group once more and we were given notes and pens. On average I was now getting a new pen everyday and had contemplated starting a stationery outlet. The whiteboard at the end of the room had the words 'Stress Management' and 'Self Esteem' written in large black text.

The private health insurance companies were helping financially to provide resources such as pens and relevant notes, and exercise books. My introductory pack consisted of papers describing my responsibilities and the working rules of the unit. I was also given a ruler. Sonia had stated the reasons for such funding – it was cost-effective, reducing patient admission and therefore lessening the cost of health services. I wondered if my monthly insurance payments would decrease in light of that.

Guy had made an appearance and Joy was sitting opposite him. John was not present but I understood his reasons for not wanting to participate.

'Gardenia, could you find John? I think he's in his bedroom,' Sonia said.

I acquiesced to authority and found John sitting on his bed. He was looking at the daily paper.

'Just finding out where the garage sales are situated,' he said.

I saw a very large cloth bag, sitting on his bed. I looked around the room; it was a mess. Clothes were haphazardly arranged, with unusual items chaotically displayed. A growing teaspoon collection was forming on his bedside table and a pile of *National Geographic* magazines were growing in the corner of the room. Old black and white photos of various portraits of men in full uniform were sitting on his desk. An assortment of lollies in packets, chips unopened and various foodstuffs were scattered on the floor. A big selection of books on war was also piled near his desk.

He could do with buying something necessary at garage sales, like decent clothes, bedding, soaps, hair shampoo and underwear, but can you get those things there? He definitely needs them.

'We're having a group therapy class – you have to go,' I said.

John nodded and obeyed, following me with his cane tapping on the floor.

We entered the room and I saw Guy studying Joy's shirt and the silhouette of her breasts. He was laughing and I saw why he was amused. Joy did not have a bra on and her shirt was viscose synthetic georgette, meaning you could see through it. I don't think I was the only one to acknowledge her appearance but we all decided to ignore her fashion statement, as no one made any objection.

Sonia started the meeting. 'It's wonderful to see you all here,' she said.

I noticed Joy's eyelids slowly closing and opening and then they stopped moving. *She doesn't need a tranquilliser; she knows how to relax. I'm envious. Although it could be a side effect of the medication.*

'Does anyone know what self-esteem is?' Sonia said.

'Yes, I do,' said John. 'Isn't it how you think of yourself? I'm very nice at times, depending on the situation of course, even if others don't believe I'm nice.'

'What happens if other people don't think you're nice?' said Joy. 'Is your self-esteem dependent on others? If other people don't like you, it's probably because you're not very nice.'

Joy was obviously not asleep and I wondered if she was naturally devious.

'Self-esteem is how we think of ourselves. Do we place ourselves in high regard or do we dislike ourselves? If our self-esteem is high, then we think of ourselves in a positive manner,' Sonia said.

'Yes, but what happens if other people don't like you?' said Joy again. She wasn't getting the answer she wanted.

'Yeah, and what happens if the system puts you in a prison hospital and everyone thinks you're a lunatic? How are you supposed to like yourself when that happens?' said Guy.

Joy looked at him and nodded. Guy looked like a volcano, ready to erupt. It was too early in the morning for me to see Mount Vesuvius and lava spouting out of Guy's mouth.

Sonia was writing some words on the whiteboard. 'Do you remember when we talked about CBT the other day? I asked you all to think about a situation or event and what your thoughts were concerning this event? Let's look at what Guy said before. He thought that being in hospital and being locked up, so to speak, was terrifying and lowered his self-esteem.'

'I was locked up and it was frightening,' said Guy.

Sonia nodded. 'What sort of impact do you think this would have, on Guy?' she asked.

'He would feel awful and he would hate himself and think of himself as a loony,' said John.

'Thanks a lot,' said Guy.

'Can you see that it isn't the situation but how Guy interprets the event? Guy's way of understanding or his thinking isn't helpful. It makes him depressed, angry and anxious,' Sonia continued.

'Well, it would make you feel like that,' Joy said.

'What are your thoughts, Guy?' Sonia asked.

'Well, everything always goes wrong. People always let me down. I'm mad. I'm an idiot and I'm a failure.'

'Good,' said Sonia. She began writing on the whiteboard.

Errors in Thinking
1. Mind reading
2. Catastrophising
3. Labelling
4. Overgeneralising
5. Fortune telling
6. Black and white thinking

Sonia spoke in a serious manner. 'Guy's self-defeating talk is an example of errors in thinking. Are these thoughts and feelings constructive? Even if this situation or event did take place, how we respond to it affects our life. What evidence does Guy have that people always let him down? Is he really mad or bad or a failure?'

'I think there's plenty of evidence,' I said.

Joy broke into loud raucous laughter.

'Please take this seriously, for Guy's sake,' said Sonia.

'I'm not a bad person. I still have some things going for me,' said Guy.

'Even if it is true, it doesn't help thinking like that, does it?' Joy said.

'That's right, Joy. You can't change the situation or event but you can control your response. We can challenge this negative thinking. We can modify our automatic thoughts or core beliefs. Even if some of these issues are persistent, we can challenge them. We can learn new skills and form better habits,' Sonia continued. 'I've given you some sheets on structured problem solving. What are the disadvantages and advantages to your thinking? For instance, what aspects do you like about yourself, Gardenia? What traits would you like to keep and what aspects would you change for the better?'

I felt obliged to talk. I didn't want to be personal and I wanted some things kept private. 'I have some goals.'

'Good. What are they?' Sonia asked.

'I want to go to France. I want to have better clothes. They're only dreams and can never happen. I don't have the money.'

'Can anyone tell me what sort of error in thinking Gardenia has?' said Sonia.

'I don't think she's wrong. You have to have money to travel,' said Guy.

'Is she overgeneralising and fortune telling that her dreams will never come true?' Sonia said.

I feel like singing, 'Somewhere over the rainbow'.

'It might happen. Someone in her family could die and leave her a lot of money,' Joy said.

'Having a dream or goal is important but what happens if we don't achieve our goal? Or think that it's impossible to even try,' Sonia said.

'Bloody lousy,' said Guy.

'That's right. Perhaps going to France is a big leap but there are smaller goals and problem solving skills we can put into place to realise our dreams. Aren't there?'

'It's like gradually confronting our fears,' I said.

'Anything is possible,' said Joy.

'Sometimes it's not the situation or goal that is too difficult to achieve, it's our belief system that needs to be understood. If we can control and understand our thinking, overcome fears or irrational ideas, then anything is possible. I would like you to write down some situations or circumstances that you find difficult. It can be in your everyday life or, if you feel more adventurous, a situation that causes a negative reaction or emotion. It can be in the past or the present or future. How did this situation make you feel? And then I want you to recognise if you have any errors in thinking. Can you give me an example, John?'

'I don't like leaving the house, even to go to the local shops.'

'Why is that, John? What are your thoughts?'

'I don't know. I'm just scared.'

'There's a thought going through your mind that creates this fear. This therapy is not easy, especially just understanding it for the first time. Perhaps a good idea might be to keep a diary and to write down your thoughts,' said Sonia. 'We're going to break for morning tea and afterwards we're going to go through some relaxation techniques. You're all doing very well and showing a great deal of courage. I congratulate you.'

I poured my fifth cup of coffee for the morning and took a biscuit from the barrel. Joy, Guy and John followed suit and then joined me in the garden. We sat under the veranda and I watched John take his tobacco pouch out from his shirt pocket and roll a cigarette. Joy had a packet of tailor-made cigarettes and also proceeded to draw in the nicotine substance. I had not seen her have a cigarette before.

'I did give it up but I'm so stressed I've taken it up again,' she said.

'I gave it up but it's hard,' said Guy.

I saw him looking at the remains of a cigarette stub in the ashtray. *I wonder if he's going to pick it up. I've seen worse things happen.*

'Would you like a cigarette, Guy?' Joy said.

'No, I'm okay, I'm getting stronger.'

'Cigarettes are getting more expensive by the day,' Joy said.

I looked at the table. It was disgustingly littered with dirty used cups, saucers, soft drink cans, and lolly wrappers. I watched flies descend and retrieve morsels of food. I thought about getting a tray from the kitchen and cleaning the rubbish. I read the notice on the outside wall – 'Return all dirty dishes to kitchen.' *That's a fat lot of good. Obviously no one takes this message seriously. It's not my duty to clean up after others, is it?*

I looked at them puffing away with remorse and a paradoxical sense of pleasure. I had given up the addiction a few years ago but I still longed for the chemical fix. John had finished his rollie and I watched him pick up a cigarette stub from the ground. He straightened it and put it in his mouth and lit it, breathing in its fumes. *He must have run out of tobacco, but he isn't going to bludge a cigarette from Joy. He goes up in my estimation.*

'I think you could be a model,' John said looking at me.

What's he after? I had thought about being beautiful, but had decided against it. I wanted to be known for my intelligence.

'They have models that are fatter, these days,' John continued.

I smiled. I was not going to be nasty any more. Not to John, no matter what he said. After all, it only made me feel guilty. He was sick and I felt that a negative response would only aggravate his illness, whatever that was. I was starting to believe I had a purpose. The possibility of helping those who were inflicted with mental problems was like a bud inside my brain, ready to blossom.

'I'm having a coffee. Do you want one?' I asked John.

'Yes, please.'

'Do you want one too, Joy?' I said.

'Yes, please.'

'How do you have it, John?' I asked.

'Black, sweet and hot, just like my women,' John answered.

I bit my lip and smiled at him. I had decided not to ask Guy because acts of kindness needed to be taken step by step. If I did too much for others, I would resent it and then give up on my purpose. I had listened to Sonia's speech on errors in thinking and goals that had to be realistic.

I passed Sonia in the kitchen. I took two discoloured white cups from the cupboard. I placed a saucer under each one. *Nice to have a fresh mug, isn't it?* I pressed the button on the kettle and waited for it to boil.

I imagined John having a sexual encounter with his hot, black, sweet woman. The image made me feel sick. I wondered how she could even contemplate being in bed with him. I felt like I was an accomplice in some debauched pornographic film. *I am a bad person. This is proof of it.*

I tried very hard to walk and not spill the liquid into the saucers. It was unavoidable as I juggled with the two cups and the fly screen door. *They could at least help. It's not as if they can't see me.*

'Sorry about that,' I said, putting the cup in front of John.

'That's okay,' John said as he poured the liquid in the saucer back into his cup. He slurped his coffee.

I wanted to say he was a disgusting pig but stopped myself. *I'm a bitch but then I haven't done anything wrong. I didn't say it, did I?*

'You're a nice person, Gardenia,' he said.

If only he really knew.

'Makes a change, doesn't it? Better than being in hospital. Have time to rest and get it all together,' John said.

'Depression is a horrid thing, isn't it?' I said. I didn't want to tell them my own personal history. That I had hallucinations of devils telling me to go to hell. I couldn't say I had been delusional and paranoid, but then John would understand.

'You have everything,' said Joy, looking at me. 'You have beautiful hands and a good-looking head. You're intelligent and I bet you're good at everything. You could have anyone you want.'

'I like John.' I was being nasty again. 'I'm sorry, John.'

He grimaced, showing only two teeth in his mouth. I looked at him and wondered how he could eat. He wouldn't be able to chew anything. *Perhaps he wears dentures and has forgotten to put them in this morning. He reminds me of a rabbit.*

'I've got cancer,' said John.

Bloody hell, that's a cheer-up.

'That's awful,' said Joy. 'How bad is it?'

'Pretty bad.'

'Well, you're here now. You're not stuck to any tubes. Looks like you'll make it,' I said.

'It's in remission.'

'Well, there you go, it's not that bad,' I said.

I thought that every word I spoke had a distinct evil flavour. *Here he is nearly dead and all I can think about is me and how shitty my life is. But then I'm just like a dead spirit meandering around a hospital ward.* I understood why John kept on talking about lost spirits, floundering in space. He knows he's going to die.

'Well, it's not all bad, is it?' I felt uncomfortable, especially around someone who was seriously ill. He did look old. 'You've had a good life.

I mean you have lived to a good age. You still have lots going for you. Would you like another cup of coffee?'

'No, I think I'll just lie on my bed for a while and read a magazine.' John limped to the kitchen door.

'Did you know that the word okay is the most frequently used word in the English language?' Guy said.

Did he just hear our conversation?

Joy looked at him and nodded. 'I like your top and it matches your pants, Gardenia,' said Joy. 'Do you like it?'

'I think your top looks good too,' said Guy,

'Yes, I do like it,' I said. I thought it was best to agree.

'I like your hair too,' Joy said. 'Do you dye it or is it naturally that red colour?'

I wondered if the comment was meant to be insulting or appreciative. I had some sympathy for Joy. I knew she had problems.

'I'd rather watch Foxtel, wouldn't you?' Guy said. 'Do you know when this meeting is supposed to finish?'

'I don't know everything. Maybe you should ask Sonia,' Joy said.

'Okay, settle down. I was just making conversation.'

'I think it finishes at three o'clock,' I said.

'Thanks. What's for tea?'

'It says on the noticeboard. Can't you figure out anything?' Joy said.

Joy was being aggressive and I knew why. John was seriously ill. *She is afraid of her own mortality. Or maybe she likes him.*

'You need anger management therapy, Joy,' Guy said and he went back inside the house.

'I'm going to clean this ashtray. It looks hideous,' Joy said.

The ashtray consisted of a small terracotta bowl with sand in it. Joy took the sifting tool that was on the floor and poured the sand through it to another bowl. She then took the sifted sand and poured it back into the ashtray. The butts and pieces of scrunched-up paper that were left in the sifter Joy disposed of in the rubbish bin.

'It would be scary, if you put it in the bin and the cigarette was still burning,' I said, trying to make light conversation. 'I suppose they think we'll burn the place down.'

'Do you think I would burn this place down? Do you think I'm that stupid?'

'No,' I said. I wanted to get away from Joy and her misery but realised I couldn't run away from everything.

'I have some washing to do later on. Would you like me to do yours as well?' I said. I wanted to tell Joy to go to hell and then I wanted to yell obscenities at the others and walk out the front door, never to return.

I saw Guy at the kitchen window. His face was squashed up against the glass pane. He looked like a bank robber, disguised, using a stocking as a mask.

I wonder if he's watching Joy, trying to memorise the sequence of sifting and putting the rubbish in the right place. But he doesn't smoke. He might want to help clean. I have an imaginative mind. He's probably not thinking that at all.

'I think we better go in,' I said.

The next session comprised of learning two relaxation techniques. The first was a progressive muscle relaxation. Each muscle in the body was clenched, made tense then let go to relax. Beginning at the toes and feet, going up through the lower body to the arms, hands, fingers and then to the facial features. We were sitting in hard-backed plastic chairs and I wondered if such amenities helped the process.

Soft music played in the background. Dolphin and whale noises were heard as Sonia talked about recognising tension.

'Where is this tension, what part of the body? What does it feel like and how did the tension occur?'

I felt depressed, and learning about John's illness didn't help. I tried to imagine something positive and constructive while I was under the hypnotic spell of Sonia's Scottish accent. I visualised sitting under the veranda and I fantasised about the dark-haired, good-looking man again. He was standing under the willow tree, watching me. I pretended to ignore his constant staring. His eyes were bright, sparkling. He was wearing a blue shirt and white pants. *Wasn't Guy wearing the same outfit my first day at Pine View?* I watched the man place a blanket on the ground and take a bottle of wine and glasses from a wicker basket and he waved to me. *I wonder what he's after. Probably just sex.*

The scene reminded me of a painting by Renoir, with pastel colours emerging and blending. I thought of the painters Manet and George Seurat and their depictions of figures in the landscape enjoying a picnic. The artist Seurat used a pointillist technique and I imagined his painting of women and men strolling in the park, with their splendid gowns and umbrellas that protected them from the sun. *He must have been an obsessive chap. Fancy doing a large painting with tiny dots. It took him years. He must have had good concentration skills, as well as patience.*

The second technique was called mindfulness. This was an exercise where the mind concentrated on a vision of one particular object or a singular thought. If the thought or imagined object was no longer in the mind's eye, then concentration was needed to recover it. I found the exercise very powerful and useful. The distraction from my usual anxiety and worries relaxed my mind.

Sonia outlined the topics to be discussed in future sessions. The studies would relate to concepts of assertive and non-assertive behaviour. Goal-setting and problem-solving techniques would also be continual subjects to be analysed. The automatic thoughts related to situations needed to be understood – the event, thought and feeling.

We were given homework, to write our thoughts in a journal. We were to analyse our thinking and the reasons behind our judgements. Sonia liked to use the word 'evidence'.

'Is it likely that Joy will be hit by a truck if she walks out into the street? It might be a possibility, but is it likely?' Sonia wanted us to write one ABC per day. She wanted us to continue trying to understand cognitive behaviour therapy. She wrote in black text on the whiteboard.

    A – Situation
    B – Thought
    C – Feeling

The group acknowledged Sonia's help, with everyone saying thank you, me included. It was three o'clock and the group dispersed.

At teatime, I told Sonia that I wouldn't be attending the groaning group. I was not interested in listening to other people complain, so I made my apologies, saying I had a headache and needed rest. It wasn't a lie as such but a necessary thing to do. It was time out for me, lessoning the impact of my new situation and the clients who lived with me.

7

I woke up the next morning, which was unfortunate, because I wanted to remain unconscious, but my mind had other ideas. While it was an involuntary act on behalf of my brain to rise and shine with a new day, I was sceptical about its decision. I disliked the idea of thinking, making decisions, finding a purpose. I wanted life easy. It was a question of either doing something with my life or not doing anything. I looked at my world in black and white. Good or bad, ugly or beautiful, sad or happy.

I looked at myself in the mirror. I brushed my hair, trying to make it look feminine. I put on my jeans and long T-shirt, some drop earrings and my sandshoes. I went downstairs to face another day.

I had my X-rays, the EGG and the CAT scan. I was and wasn't frightened. Having tests was the norm for me, but I did care about the result. Many of the tests I had undergone were related to my medication, finding out the chemical levels in my body. Today I was to see the neurologist. An appointment had been made and I took a taxi to the specialist's rooms. I was given a taxi voucher and was thankful for that. The medical clinic wasn't far away, opposite the Queen Victoria hospital. The modern clinic had a number of specialists. I went to the reception desk and stated my name and the doctor I was to see.

'I'm here for my appointment, my name is Gardenia Baxter and I'm to see a Doctor Evans.'

'Yes, Professor Evans.' The receptionist looked at her computer. 'Do you have your Medicare card and any concession cards?'

'Yes.' I passed the two cards to her. I think she noted the numbers and expiry dates.

'Take a seat. He'll be with you shortly.'

I sat down and waited. Two other men were in the reception area. One was looking at a magazine and the other one was looking at his mobile phone. I had my X-rays with me and it was not long before the specialist appeared.

'Hello, I'm Professor Evans. Nice to meet you.'

He put out his hand and I shook it firmly. I was told a weak handshake meant a weak character.

'Follow me,' he said.

I walked into his room and sat on the chair next to his desk.

'So you've been having some falls.'

'Yes.'

'Your psychiatrist Dr Jarvie and Doctor Green wanted me to see you to find out what's going on.'

I nodded.

'I just want to take some details. Gardenia Baxter, that's your name.'

I nodded.

'Born 31 August 1964.'

I nodded again.

'So what are these falls like?'

'I shake, like an involuntary jerk. I see my arms moving around, and sometimes when I continually jerk like that, I have a blackout. I fall down and lose consciousness for a second.'

'Do you feel dazed, groggy afterwards?'

'No, I remember falling, like everything is in slow motion. I put my arms out to protect myself.'

'Have you had these falls before?'

'Yes, not long ago when I was at Felixstowe psychiatric hospital.'

'Were those falls the same as you're having now?'

'Yes. At Felixstowe, my arms were shaking like they are now. It's a very surreal experience. I blacked out for a few seconds.'

'You lost consciousness.' Doctor Evans was being very thorough.

I only hoped I could give him the right information for him to make a diagnosis.

'When I was at home a few years ago, I was on a ladder outside, trying to retrieve some boxes that were on top of a wardrobe. I blacked out and fell on the ground. I hit my head on the cement and there was blood everywhere.'

'Did you notice your arm shaking?'

'Yes.'

'What arm was it that shook, left or right?'

'It was my left arm, but it was a long time ago, so I'm not sure. I think it was more like a jerking movement. I also have a stammering problem. I'ave only noticed it in the last couple of days. I say the same word a number of times. It's very frustrating and makes me feel self-conscious.'

'Yes, I have noticed it. I want to examine you. Can you take off your pink shoes and sit on the bed.'

I sat on the edge of the bed and the professor put his finger in front of my face.

'I want you to follow this finger.' He moved his finger sideways, then up and down. 'Now I want you to touch your nose with your finger, and then touch my finger.'

I did so and wondered if I was doing the tests correctly.

'I want you to say, la, la, la la as quick as you can, over and over.' The doctor looked in my mouth. 'Say AHHH. Can you hear this?' The professor whispered into my ear the number thirty-six and then whispered into my other ear the number twenty-six.

'Now I'm just going to look into the back of your eye. Look behind me at the painting on the wall.' He shone a torch into my eyes. 'Now with your thumb, touch your fingers. Do that quickly, and now with your other hand. Now can you lie on the bed. Put your arms up and I want you to press with your hand against my hand.'

I felt my strength pressing against his hand.

'Now use your other hand.'

He then touched my palm. It was like a tickle. 'Can you feel that?'

'Yes.' *This is a complex examination. What does it mean?*

He did the same thing with my other hand, tickling my palm. 'Now I'm going to touch your feet.'

I felt a ticklish feathery touch on the soles of both feet.

Then the professor used a rubber-type instrument on the bottom of my feet, my knees and my elbows.

He's testing my reflexes.

'Okay, you can get down now. Can you walk down this hallway, away from me.'

I did what was I was told.

'Now stop and walk back.'

I noticed my arms were straight at my sides.

'Now let's look at the X-rays.'

I thought Professor Evans would look at the X-rays I had brought with me. Instead, he was able to access the X-ray imaging on the computer. I remembered the CAT scan, lying on a bed and moving into a tunnel-like machine. I saw the images generated on the professor's computer. I could see the shape of my brain, in my skull. It was monotone in parts, with grey and black areas.

The professor clicked on different images, zooming in and out. 'Well, that's good,' He turned away from the screen. 'You have a normal brain, no sign of tumours or scars. How long have you been on lamotragine?'

'Several years.'

'Did you take it as a mood stabiliser or an anticonvulsant?'

'I think both. Is it epilepsy?'

'Yes, I think it is.'

I was sure these seizures were related to my medication.

'You do have epilepsy. It's idiopathetic. It means that the cause is so small, you can't see it.'

If you can't see it, then how do you know?

'The medication which you're on can cause seizures. I'm going to increase your Lamotragine and I want you to take another anticonvulsant, benztropine.'

Oh no, not more tablets, but at least my brain is normal.

The professor stood up and shook my hand. 'It was very nice to meet you,' he said.

I went back to Pine View via taxi. I thought of the outcome of the tests. I should have asked more questions. *Will the benztropine help and will I have any more seizures?* It was obvious that he was treating the epilepsy, but it was all due to side effects.

I found Joy in the kitchen, standing, looking out of the window. Her back was facing me, so I don't think she was aware of my presence. I could hear her talking. I noticed some small dolls sitting on the window sill.

'Well, what are you saying to me then?' she said.

Is she talking to me? I looked at the dolls and they reminded me of leprechauns dressed in weird costumes.

'What? I can't hear you,' she said. She must have received an answer because she responded with, 'Go and get stuffed.'

'What in the world are they?' I said, hoping to distract Joy from a life that would only end in tears.

'They're trolls,' she said. 'They help me.'

Obviously.

'How do they help you, Joy?' I was beginning to feel like the resident psychologist.

'I talk to them and their different personalities come to life. They influence me and help me to get out more and socialise and be happy.'

Do the trolls go out everyday? We're all different and if it works, why question it? I was curious. There must be some complicated therapy involved. 'How do you make them come alive?'

'Well, you give them names and you speak to them, like they're people,' said Joy.

'Like having a dog.'

'Yes, and they talk back to you too,' said Joy.

'So how do they help?' *It might not be a bad idea.*

'Each doll plays a role and by changing their small costumes, I can also change their identity. See this troll here?'

Joy showed me the plastic figurine. It had bright blue tufts of hair sprouting from its head. Its glass eyes, coupled with a disfigured nose, made it look frightening. I looked at the other trolls. They were ugly and their expressions signified they were undergoing some form of torture. *Joy's connection with reality is very tenuous, but who am I to judge?*

'I use this troll when I'm sad or depressed. You see the blue hair?'

They're colour-coded.

'Its presence reminds me that I'm unhappy. It also means that I can share my problems and be understood.'

This is an abstract but practical idea to relieve despair. It makes sense.

'So that's how you become aware of a specific thought or idea that's bothering you?' I said.

'Yes, it's like a revelation,' said Joy and she placed the blue-haired creature back with its friends.

'So what's that troll for?' I asked, pointing to the creature that was dressed in green plastic, not dissimilar to the material of a tidy bin liner.'

'Well, that troll reminds me of death. I try to comprehend that death is a part of life. Being frightened of what will eventually happen affects my ability to see life now, in a good way. So I try to lessen my anxieties, understanding that life is short. I don't want to worry all the time, because we all end up buried in the earth or cremated.

Rubbish, green waste material for bins, buried and cremated remains, yes, that makes sense.

'What does that one mean?' I pointed to a troll dressed in a rag like hessian.

'Oh, that's Cinderella.'

I had some inkling as to what she was going to say but I wanted to hear her theory.

'When I get sick of cooking and cleaning, I race upstairs and realise I have something to wear and I don't feel so bad,' said Joy.

'I just have to go to the toilet, I'll be back in a minute.' I hurried to my room and shut the door. I remembered the troll-like creatures from my childhood. They were a terrifying object back then and the concept of living, talking trolls was frightening. My self-doubt about having a possible psychotic thought disorder made me distrust a talking troll therapy. I didn't want to be influenced by Joy's logical but imaginative ideas. I was also scared of people who paid money to purchase such a product. I couldn't see the attraction of their small tufts of vibrant coloured hair with bright purple, pink and blue fibres springing out of their small plastic heads.

Living in this fantastical world helps Joy to cope in a scary world. I hope they help her, although if she tells them to get stuffed, they can't be that nice?

I realised this environment did not encourage personal growth or increase self-esteem, even though the therapy classes did try to instil these positive beliefs. To be bombarded with other people's problems constantly was like being in an emergency psychiatric ward. I knew that reintegrating the 'mentally ill' back into society was a form of social conditioning. *I'm a new product being exposed to the market, a design on a production line, a risky venture. Will I be successful?*

It had been a fortnight since my arrival at Pine View. The time had passed slowly and I was eager to leave. The residential rehab programme was supposed to run for two months. Whether I could leave the premises was in question, as I had given my permission to participate. Signatures on forms had a threatening finality.

I tried to be positive and to believe that the lowering of the antipsychotic had made an impact. I noticed the sedative effects had decreased and my ability to think had improved. To be able to concentrate, without continually going to my bed to rest, gave me a new lease on life, a sense of hope that life could get better. I wanted to believe that the decrease in the tranquillisers were the cause of this. I also wanted to believe that the antidepressants were working. It was the only rational hope I had, to understand my position, my confusion, my time at Felixstowe and why I was defined and categorised as mentally ill.

I was becoming conscious of a new world and this journey into uncharted waters was frightening and liberating at the same time. It was difficult opening cans of worms when you didn't want to go fishing.

I also noticed my mood changing from one extreme to another. I would have a positive outlook and think constructively and then a few hours later become depressed and angry with life's futility. Perhaps this was a normal reaction to my situation or a normal everyday response that happened to people everywhere, on occasion. My plight was related to my circumstances. If I did anything that was a little out of the ordinary or not understood by the programme initiators, then it was due to my illness. It was going to be a long road to challenge this, to prove my innocence, that my emotions were normal.

Sometimes I did want more tablets to block out my feelings of helplessness, but I always held the hope that my life would be profoundly different in time. Like Joy, fantasies played a big part in this, as an escape, a life force that gave me a future. The idea of happiness was an engineering concept I would have to create. If misery existed, then pleasure must be conceivable?

The cognitive therapy did help my awareness of self. It was a case of taking responsibility. I had long ago given up the idea of telling my doctors that I was not ill, because they just didn't believe me. I was told that I had to accept my problems and so I did.

It was a pivotal point in my life knowing I would not be burnt at the stake for having a different opinion. Whatever had happened in the past, trauma from Felixstowe or their current diagnosis or label, I still had control over my mind. The therapy of CBT had actually released me from my despair. It gave me the opportunity to see life differently. My belief in self did not come easily nor did it happen overnight.

I felt I had to accept an illness that I had acquired from a mental health system. Also I had to question its validity and therefore the authority that brought it into being. It was in not accepting my state and my environment that the possibility of having a better quality of life became real.

I was to see Doctor Green again. Sonia said he would arrive in the next half an hour. I wanted to ask some relevant questions, like what was wrong with me. I was waiting in the lounge room when I heard a knock on the door. I could surmise that the doctor had arrived. Doctor Green did not look terrifying, as I was getting used to his frog-like appearance.

'I have some questions,' I said.

'Yes, go on. I'll try to answer them to the best of my ability.'

'Many of these medications I take have side effects, don't they?' I knew he didn't appreciate me asking such a question, but it was a serious subject and I had to know. 'They can make you constipated, can't they?' I could not forget my weekly enemas both in hospital and as an outpatient, or the humiliation and effect they had on me.

'Yes that can happen,' the doctor said. 'Let's talk about how you're going now. We don't have to go over the past again.'

I ignored him. 'Can medication give you high cholesterol and diabetes?' I asked.

'Yes, some medications can do that.'

'I never heard voices before. It was because I couldn't sleep. I don't think I have a psychotic disorder. Can sleeping tablets lose their effect over time?'

'Yes, they are addictive,' the doctor answered. 'I think you have a schizoaffective disorder.'

I felt my heart stop for a second and then return to its rhythmic beating. I didn't like his appraisal or the word that aptly described insanity.

'I think my problem is related to post-traumatic stress disorder. If I have to keep on saying to myself repeatedly, "It's going to be all right," I must be in fear.'

I know he'll reply with an abstract answer, undermining my opinion.

'I can't say in hindsight,' the doctor replied.

'I took sleeping tablets both night and day for three years after I came out of Felixstowe, so I could forget the traumatic experience. If sleeping tablets are addictive, then it's understandable. The tablets lost their potency and that's why I couldn't sleep and why I was psychotic.'

'I can understand that you'e upset but we have to work out your present problems.'

'What medication did they give me at Felixstowe?' I asked. I knew that my questions about the negligence of a psychiatric system were confrontational, so I had to be smart. 'I want to find out what the medications are for, so I can understand my problem.' I wanted to find out what the side effects were.

'Do you think it's a good idea to put on the white coat, Gardenia? Reiterating the past doesn't take you forward.'

'The past has never left me and I know I'm allowed to see my notes because of the Freedom of Information Act that was passed in 1991.'

I think he knew I wasn't bluffing. My anger at having to justify my sanity gave me courage. I had the right to see my notes and want to understand my past.

'Okay, I'll tell you.' He looked at my file, going through the individual papers. He looked worried. 'You were on many medications at different times and with different dosages. Haloperidol, Perphenazine, fluphenazine, orphenadrine, lorazepam, temazepam, carbamazepine, benztropine, lithium, prothiaden, zoloft, epilem, chlorpromazine, thioridazine, clonazepam, stelazine, and alprazolam.'

I tried to write down the names. I had brought a notebook, for that reason. 'I'm sorry. I have no idea of the spelling. Can you write them down for me?' *The computer at the library will give me information; that's if I have the right spelling.*

Doctor Green wrote down the many medications. I was not surprised by the amount and the variety. I could not easily forget the daily ritual of taking medication.

'Why did they put me in a secure ward? Was it because I ran home?'

'It's important to have this type of facility, so a patient doesn't harm themselves or others,' he said.

He has a gentle manner even when discussing prison-type confinement. I wonder if he's threatened by me questioning his practice.

'How can I be psychotic if I know my way home? I ran away from the Felixstowe hospital. I had to return because of detaining orders. They put me in high security afterwards. Doesn't psychosis mean you're living in an unreal world?'

'You can be psychotic and know the real world too,' he said.

God, they have an answer for everything, when it suits them.

'I know it must be difficult and I understand your anger but sometimes we have to accept our problems.'

Everyone keeps on telling me to accept I'm a moron.

'But I wasn't going to harm anyone and I wasn't going to harm myself. I just wanted to go home and I didn't want to be in Felixstowe.'

'They said you didn't have enough insight to understand your need for treatment,' the doctor said.

It's a lost cause.

Trembling, I left the doctor. It took a lot of courage to say what I had been thinking for the last seven years. My fear was such that I asked Sonia for another tablet. She gave it to me, no questions asked. Medication was required for an illness.

Over and over in my mind, the same idea was repeating itself. They were saying I was insane. *Good reference for a job.*

I wanted to tell the doctor a lot more but I didn't think he was up to it. I wanted to say I was sick of nurses and other health professionals asking me repeatedly if I was hearing voices or seeing things. I wanted to say that my lack of concentration wasn't because I was sick in the mind. I wanted to say my fear and panic was not a delusion.

Is it any wonder I have lost trust in myself and everyone in society? Instead of helping me, they have done exactly the opposite. If I was so sick, then why did I recover at home? I'm sure they would have an answer for that. I was in remission.

So I did what I was planning to do – visit the local library. The facility looked like a renovated church and it was an interesting place. I loved the fact that you didn't have to pay money to read a book. There were parts of the building that had extensions added. I looked through the different rooms and saw the different categories. I did not know where to start and wondered what would be of interest.

My first thought was an economic one. *What do I need for my survival?*

I knew psychology would be a useful subject, but I wasn't interested in theories. I wondered about reincarnation and the mind. *Do they have an alternative section with philosophy, or new age books?*

I wanted to be reassured, for someone to say, 'I know exactly what you're going through.' I wanted to interact with people and to construct my own ideas and to make connections. I thought it better to do this by reading, rather than jumping in the deep end and actually having a conversation. I wasn't ready for that. I felt like I was reinventing myself and therefore I had to start on the ground floor. I felt like I was living a fantasy, a fiction created so I could resume a structured life.

I saw the literary fiction section and remembered how I once enjoyed reading, visualising pictures from words. I looked at the novels I had read in the past but had now forgotten. This included the classics like E.M. Forster, *A Passage to India*. Novelists like Thomas Hardy, John Steinbeck, Henry James, George Bernard Shaw, and Oscar Wilde. I loved reading *Hamlet*, standing on top of the school desk reciting, 'To be or not to be.' I read Sylvia Plath's *The Bell Jar* and works by Virginia Woolf, but I didn't want to read subjects that would remind me of my own trauma.

I did try to go back to my university texts after Felixstowe and to read about society and economical rationalism. The reasons why there is a gap between the rich and the poor. I had enjoyed reading the reference books at university. It had given me a belief system, understanding that multinationals were companies only interested in exploitation. Capitalism and the Protestant ethic were subjects that interpreted modern Western society. Now it was difficult to concentrate on a sentence. To navigate the long complex paragraphs and to try and understand the meanings was like a form of torture. It made me aware of my disability, my present circumstances and my inadequate memory.

I searched through the technical medical books and self-help publications. There were books describing various disorders and their related symptoms. Management of anxiety and depression, understanding the grief process were just a few of the subjects on show. There were basically two schools of thought when it came to relieving such problems. There was of course the medical, which was based on neurology and chemicals. There was the alternative belief that used holistic types of remedy. My problem was ideological. I had trusted the health system, their humanitarian ideology, but they had destroyed my soul.

I took the book that described the grief process. I thought it adequately described my feelings. It was a simple answer but it made sense. I didn't like the books that told personal stories of mental illness. Ideas of insanity, of individuals lost, forsaken by society were too much to digest. Reading about their pain would make me recall my time in the prison structure of Felixstowe. The hell I experienced in the paradoxical authoritarian mental health system. I would relive every moment, every fear and every imagined outcome. I would be there again, being molested by a nurse, watched by teams of doctors and nurses, inspected and interrogated. Having to live with disturbed individuals who were going through their own private hell was counter-productive to any form of recovery. Seeing electrified fences and told you were being cared for by a health system, doctors who wanted you to have a better life. I think this last idea was the most frightening.

Can self-help books change my life? They could give me courage and direction. Why do I have to change anyway? Do I have to accept an illness, to say I'm sick, but I am in a situation I cannot ignore? Then how do I get better? Is it a case of forgiveness? Did I do something wrong?

Meanings, concepts, arguments, ideas, terminology, ethics, they were all subjective and therefore there was not a right or wrong answer. I felt like I was an alien from another universe trying to understand the world of human beings. It was hard work to learn to make associations, to understand how the human mind worked.

I decided to take another book by Carl Jung and to read his ideas on the collective unconscious. The idea of interpretation of dreams as symbols could define my waking life. I could understand my problems like a fortune teller could explain my present and future. *Perhaps analyse my birth chart.*

I thought about my art work and if that held possibilities for therapy. A process of creativity was a process of change and if it could be done on paper then why not in the mind?

I made my way to the computer. I now had access to the worldwide web and I was going to try and get as much information as I could. It would be confronting to know just what medication I had been on and why, but I had to do it. It was a form of acceptance, after all.

I saw that there were three computers and luckily there was one free space. The computers at the library near my home were always booked out.

I looked at my list of long words and then I searched the appropriate sites. I discovered I had been taking six types of antipsychotics during my time at Felixstowe. Included were two types of mood stabilising drugs and two types of antidepressants. Additionally three types of muscle relaxants or medications to offset the side effects of the antipsychotics were included. Also four types of anti-anxiety medications.

My horror was justified as I began to unravel the medical definitions and uses and their side effects. The trauma I experienced at Felixstowe was largely due to the side effects of these medications. I knew that there could be adverse side effects to all medications but this was in another league. My turmoil at seeing all this in black and white made me feel grateful that I was in a library. I couldn't scream and get upset because I would get kicked out. So onward I went, doing my best to concentrate and not cry.

There were numerous accounts of adverse effects such as constipation, dry mouth and blurred vision and these were just the unwanted effects of the antidepressants. It didn't take me long to remember my enemas or my wearing magnified glasses that made my eyes look like they had just popped out of a bottle.

The antipsychotics had a line-up of affects that a hypochondriac would die for. Some of the more interesting ones that I related to and could tick off as applying to me were the Parkinsonian affects. They included tremors, shaking and the continual trembling of my fingers and hands. The restlessness and the intense pain I felt with my legs wanting to move all the time was a common adverse effect of the antipsychotics. *Internal torture would not even come close to describing it.*

I ticked the boxes describing pacing the floors, jerking of the muscles of the face, neck, trunk and extremities. I remembered all of these horrible and painful things happening. How could I forget? I experienced dizziness and falling over, tripping on the pavement. That was due to the sedative effects of the major tranquillisers. I couldn't pick up my feet. My vomiting each morning as they carried me to the showers was also due to the medication and my menstrual changes were another effect. I remembered not having a period for six months and they thought I was pregnant and tests were carried out just to make sure. Paralysis was another effect and I remembered the time when I couldn't move my head and they quickly gave me an injection of Benztropine. That was called dystonia.

The actions which had haunted me over the years and made me think I had really lost my sanity were described in these articles. The acrobatic movements I remembered performing in the secure ward were called 'choreoathetosis movements'. This was a side effect of lithium. My disrobing or undressing, which I thought was a part of my illness, was a condition that was caused by medication too. I remembered the doctor saying that I was very sensitive and only now I realised his meaning. I was sensitive to their medication. The odd faces I was pulling at different times and the worming movement of my tongue was also due to the effects of these drugs.

Did they never at the time consider how the drugs were affecting me or were they aware I was over-medicated and as such were negligent in their treatment? Obviously if they did, they didn't do anything about it. Perhaps as student doctors they didn't realise?

My feeling at this point in time was 'it's all too late'. My problems had stemmed from their mismanagement and not an organic illness. *No wonder Doctor Jarvie wanted to apologise.*

Reading about the medications and the causes of my distress was like going back in time and feeling it all over again. Except I wasn't there, I was in a library. I kept on with my research. It was a question of dignity.

I continued to tick the boxes. Increased sweating, yes, that was continual except when I didn't sweat at all and had to take cold showers every five minutes on sweltering hot summer days. My difficulty in urinating and urinary retention, well, that would explain having to have the catheters.

Other antipsychotic side effects included depression, hostility, agitation, aggression, hyperactivity, temper tantrums and other distressing feelings that would describe my time in Felixstowe. *They probably thought these side effects were symptoms of my disorder.*

Then I found out that certain types of antipsychotics lowered the threshold of epilepsy. *That's why I had the seizures, because I had never suffered epilepsy before.*

I read further and discovered that the muscle relaxants and other drugs were given to me because of the Parkinsonian effects with tremors and stiffness and also epilepsy. My walking stiffly without swinging my arms looking like a zombie was not because I was insane. My disorientation, disturbed concentration, excitement, fatigue, inability to sleep were not because I had a mental illness. My dilated pupils didn't mean I was some kind of monster. My lack or loss of coordination when I couldn't pick up a pen were not due to my own disturbed way of thinking. The tingling pins and needles in my arms and legs were not because I wasn't doing enough exercise. *Why didn't they tell me?*

My restless dancing in the music room was not due to mood swings, I was distressed and uncomfortable. My body was crying out for relief. *Is it any wonder I wanted to run away because I was frightened? What was their reason for giving me such drugs? Because I did not know who I was in a metaphorical sense? I suffered an acute anxiety crisis due to an abortion. Did they think they were doing me a favour?*

I felt like I was reading a comedy of errors but this was life and very serious. How many other lives had been destroyed because of their incompetence? How many are suffering now?

I wanted to contact a lawyer. I thought of all the euphemisms I could think of. I was going to 'take them to the cleaners'. I was going to 'suck them dry', 'throw the book at them', and 'they wouldn't have a leg to stand on'. I was going to 'make them pay'.

I had to suffer so they could make me well? I still couldn't get around that ideological concept. It just didn't make sense. I understood my problems now were directly linked to the medical system's abuse of power. I was socially withdrawn, suffering from depression, continually frightened, hostile and distrustful. Now I knew why.

Just imagine if I try to come off the tablets now, with the withdrawal effects. The chemicals change the mind's perception but I will have to be psychologically strong to attempt such an endeavour. So what now? I knew I had to come off the medication. Not only because of my weight gain, and other odd physical manifestations, but I had to prove to them I was not psychotic.

That is hard evidence and can they disprove that? Do I have the capacity to withdraw from serious medication without support? I know I will not get help. They will not encourage me to stop taking tablets. They will say if I do, I will get sick again. They have the power to force me to take medication, I know that much. They have already made up their mind. I will have to do it on my own.

I left the library remembering the words I had read in the articles. It was supposed to be common practice for physicians to tell their patients about side effects of medication. I suppose it has only come into favour because of lawsuits. Also, only experienced psychiatric doctors should attempt to treat the side effects of medication.

I walked back to the halfway house and tried to think constructively about my situation, which was not an easy thing to do. I had been overwhelmed by this knowledge. I was angry that I had been treated in such a manner but relieved at the same time. I was glad, knowing that I was not medically insane. But the experiences of the past, my memory and continued apprehension did not fade with this new-found understanding.

8

I was sitting outside under the veranda with John. I wondered if the events at Felixstowe had taken place. Was there a man without fingers or did a nurse molest me? Was I psychotic and if so did I imagine these things? It was one thing to say that side effects or being over-medicated made me crazy, but it was another thing to live with the fact. I knew John had been hospitalised at Felixstowe.

'When you were in Felixstowe, do you remember a man without fingers?' I said.

I knew John was thinking because he tapped his cane on the ground several times. I think it was an involuntary action on his behalf. It always occurred when he spoke.

'Yes, I do. His name was Frank, I think.'

Really, but then John is sick. How can I take his word for it?

'Do you remember a nurse called Luke? He had blond hair and wore glasses,' I said.

'Luke, yes, I think so. He was tall and big wasn't he, like obese?'

'Yes,' I said.

John had remembered him too. I felt a tingling sensation on my skin, like goosepimples. As if I had verified the existence of a ghost. John's response was authentication that I had not been delusional. It had happened.

'Did he do something wrong?' John's statement took me by surprise.

'Why do you say that?' I said. *Did Luke sexually assault other patients too?*

'He's a nasty piece of work, that one. Did he abuse you? I'll get my mates to deal with him,' John said.

'No, it's okay, nothing happened.'

'I can tell it did,' he said.

I didn't like the idea of violence or punishment. 'It's really a small world,' I said.

Not long after my conversation with John, I began to feel cramp-like sensations in my stomach. I told Sonia that I wasn't feeling well.

'It's probably due to all the food you've been eating. Many people have bilious attacks because they eat so much.'

Isn't food poisoning associated with stomach cramps?

The pain continued and Sonia insisted that my problem was due to indigestion.

'Just sit on the toilet. It's probably constipation,' she said.

I realised that Sonia was not taking me seriously and my pain was increasing. I took the situation in hand and rang the ambulance.

The paramedics arrived and enquired about my dilemma. They obviously knew my psychiatric history, as they spoke to Sonia about the possible cause. I was ignored. Sonia told them about my food intake and my anxiety was noted as a reason for my increasing distress and I was given another blue pill.

Soon after the ambulance left, I questioned Sonia's decision. The cramps had not abated. I knew they did not understand my physical discomfort as they viewed my distress in psychiatric terms. My only recourse was to lie on the bitumen road and scream in anguish. *If they see me as psychotic, I would at least be taken to hospital.* I knew Sonia thought my mental illness was the reason for my trauma and lying on the road was an indication of a delusional mind.

Sonia eventually understood my reality and that I was in pain. She rang the ambulance service.

The cramp in my lower torso was like a spinning washing machine that was malfunctioning. The internal pressure was like an industrial iron press flattening clothes. It would suddenly seize and sharp stabbing darts would circulate. I felt like a belt was being tightened around my waist. I was breathing like a woman in labour.

I continued to lie in the middle of the road and scream. I didn't trust Sonia or the paramedics. I had to make them believe it was an emergency.

My physical pain was serious and it was not related to my bowel actions. I didn't like the idea of being run over by a car, but I needed attention. My pain had started at three o'clock in the afternoon and it wasn't until nine o'clock that night when the second ambulance appeared.

I watched the huge vehicle back into the driveway. The lights on the van blinked and in the night its shiny polished surfaces flickered. A man and woman dressed in green paramedic suits made their way to me. I had moved to the gutter, but was going to go back to the middle of the road if they did not realise my situation.

'Hello, what's going on here, then?' The man with blond wavy hair looked at me.

I thought he sounded like an English comedian, making light of a serious situation. I knew the jovial comment was used to alleviate my feelings of terror.

'I'm not well,' I said.

'She's in a lot of pain. We called the ambulance before but we thought it wasn't that serious,' said Sonia.

'My name's Jim. So where is the pain?' The man's eyebrows were very thick and he had beautiful blue eyes.

I wonder if he's attracted to me?

'In my stomach.' I used small sentences to communicate, punctuated with loud groans.

'Okay, we'll take her in and see what's going on. Can you walk to the back of the vehicle?' he said.

I nodded. I staggered to the ambulance. I was bent over, like the hunchback of Notre Dame. I verbalised my discomfort with expletives that would have shocked a Hell's Angel bikie. I lay on the transportable bed.

'What's your name?' said the paramedic. He climbed into the back.

Obviously, the woman is going to drive.

'Gardenia Baxter.' My voice was like a whisper. I was finding it difficult to breathe.

He saw my predicament and placed a breathing apparatus over my nose and mouth. 'Here, this will make it easier.'

I knew it was oxygen and my fear subsided for a second. I watched him reading notes in a folder.

'Are you on any medications?'

'Yes, Effexor, Risperdal, Epilem and Alprazolam. Multivitamins when I can afford them.'

'Who needs multivitamins when you've got that lot?' the female driver said. She was trying to cheer me up. It didn't work.

'Anything else?' said the blue-eyed man.

'No, that's enough,' I replied.

He didn't laugh.

'We'll have to go to the Queen Victoria, it's the only one that has beds,' said the driver.

I could see the traffic lights shining in the rain. They looked like coloured glass moving and merging. Not unlike a watery foam. It reminded me of washing dishes in the kitchen sink and the detergent making a rainbow mix of bubbles.

Mum, I'll be home soon, don't worry.

'Can't we go any faster than this? Have you got the siren on?' I said.

'Try and calm down, we want to get you there in one piece.'

You have got to be joking. No, I am not going to argue with him.

I looked at the various pipes, plastic tubing, cans of chemicals, machines. I watched Jim write notes on a clipboard.

'Do you have a medical illness, like high blood pressure, diabetes?'

'I have a mental illness, schizoaffective disorder.'

'Okay, and the medications are for that?'

I nodded and squirmed around on the bed. I knew he could not give me anything to relieve my pain because they didn't know the diagnosis. 'I'm not making this up, you know,' I said.

'I do know that,' he replied. He continued to write and then he moved around the van. 'I'm just going to put this on your arm, okay?'

I nodded and watched the machine and the numbers moving, indicating my blood pressure.

'Your blood pressure is a bit high. Did you take any painkillers or panadeine forte?'

'No, just antacid,' I said.

I looked at my knight in shining armour as he wrote down the digital readings.

'You have a nice home,' he said.

I nodded. I couldn't carry on a conversation about my life in a halfway house.

'Who's your doctor?'

'Doctor Alice Jarvie, she's my psychiatrist.'

'Have you seen your doctor recently?'

'I saw her a little while ago.'

'What did she say?'

'She changed my medication,' I said. I felt restless and I wanted to get up from the bed.

The paramedic wrote down more notes and noticed my agitation.

'We'll be at the Queen Victoria in a few minutes,' the driver said.

The vehicle slowly drove through the gates of the hospital. It stopped at an entrance consisting of large glass sliding doors. The paramedics rolled the transportable bed onto the ground and wheeled me into the emergency department.

I could see faces, a blur of heads moving. *I wonder if they think I'm psychotic. Do they think I'm playacting, attention-seeking?* I screamed in anguish. *God, I'm even paranoid about having pain. As if it's my fault.*

I cried out again. 'Would you stop this? Can't you see I'm in agony? Will someone help me?'

The paramedics were talking to the emergency staff. I didn't care if they were saying I was mentally unhinged, because I knew I was not making this up. *They'll have to do something. They can't just leave me like this, can they?*

A person came up to me. I didn't know if he was a doctor or the previous paramedic who had helped me. The pain was too overwhelming for me to understand or delineate between persons, or to carry on a logical conversation.

'Don't worry,' he said. 'We'll sort you out.'

I did not trust any medical practitioners. 'Sort me out? You must be joking,' I said. I didn't care about being polite or submissive to the gods in white coats. I certainly didn't think they were useful or even good at their jobs. *They're useless oddities given positions of power. They think they're important and necessary but they're not.*

I knew that I had a slim chance of survival. I was in a life-threatening situation. I continued to scream. 'I can't go on like this. Will someone help me? If you knew what bloody pain I'm in, you would do something about it.' I had kept my control in the ambulance but my patience was wearing thin.

I felt the hospital bed moving. 'It's about time,' I said.

I was wheeled down a hallway. I passed people who were obviously curious about my dilemma.

'It's rude to stare, you know,' I yelled. *I know they're looking at me with fear and pity. Probably glad it's not them on this bed.*

I was taken to a cubicle. A long curtain of plastic sheeting surrounded me on two sides. I lay on my back with a white thermal blanket covering me. I could partly see the emergency ward. It was a hub of activity. *They're just a lot of people pretending to be busy or doing something useful.* I could see them staring at pieces of paper or standing, watching something far off. I heard the nurses talking to each other. *They're discussing their problems.* I listened to them complaining about their bad shoulders and back aches. I watched them yawn, saying they didn't get any sleep the previous night. *This is just like the television soap opera series* General Hospital. *No one is doing their job.*

'I'm not making this up, you know,'

A nurse walked past and told me off. 'Would you stop freaking out,' she said.

I was now lying on my side and gripping the rails of the bed. My hands clenched the stainless steel tubing.

A doctor eventually made an appearance. 'I'm Doctor Rousseau.'

I don't care if you're Mr Magoo.

He was a tall man with blond hair and thick-rimmed dark glasses.

'I'm in pain and I can't take this any more, okay.'

'Where is your pain?'

'In my stomach.'

He felt around and pressed some muscles.

'God help me,' I said.

'Where does it hurt? Does it hurt when I press there?' he said.

'It hurts everywhere, all the time.'

'Even there?' He continued to press my stomach in various places.

'It hurts everywhere,' I said. *Does he want me to speak in another language?*

'How long have you been in pain?'

'Since this morning,' I said.

'Okay, we better have an X ray.'

I watched Doctor Magoo walk away and talk to a group of men. 'There's probably a bloody alien in my stomach,' I cried out.

I was taken to the X-ray department and I stood in various positions as the radiologist took pictures of my pelvis, shifting me this way and that. He apologised for having to push me around so he could take the best shot, so to speak. I tried to be cooperative, but a good yell every now and then helped.

I wondered if they were worried, because the medical staff appeared unconcerned. *They should be distraught, like I am. Shouldn't they be running around? I'm going to die.*

'I won't be long now,' said the radiologist in between my cries of torment.

'If you bloody knew,' I said.

The radiologist nodded. 'I think I do know,' he replied.

Doctor Rousseau and the other doctors looked at my X-ray. I watched him getting a second, third and fourth opinion. They huddled together talking.

Am I a being from another planet with a different anatomy?

Eventually Doctor Rousseau spoke to me. 'We can't find anything in the X-rays and we're still at a loss to understand what's wrong. I think I do feel a mass but I'm not sure. I'll have a gynaecologist examine you.'

The gynaecologist was a woman and she did the same as Doctor Rousseau. She pressed and felt my stomach. 'There is a mass there,' she said.

'Thank God,' I yelled.

'We better have a CAT scan,' she said.

I was moved back and forth within the tunnel. I saw the medical staff hurry out of the room as the device had low radiation output. I could see the radiologists in an upstairs room and their faces through the glass window. They didn't look happy.

I was taken back to my previous cubicle. I waited, my body writhing in the bedclothes. I understood the difference between reality and imagination. Physical pain was real and this was not a fantasy. It was concrete. The people around me, the sounds, images and voices were like a dream. I was not asleep but living in a nightmare only comparable to the torture I experienced when I had not slept for eighteen days. I didn't want to remember my walking in the prison passage ways of Felixstowe. Nothing could be compared to that time.

I sensed my imminent death.

Doctor Rousseau came back and told me the results. 'There are two large tumours in your uterus,' he said. 'We have to operate immediately.'

I nodded.

I watched a nurse work around me. I felt the suture go into my arm. I felt giddy and sick. I was hot and feverish, sweat and perspiration was running down my face. My body was shaking. I felt my stomach being torn in all directions. It was like my body was a part of a heavyweight wrestling match. I wondered who was going to win.

I lay on the hospital bed, blubbering and making strange noises. I imagined my mother by my side, holding my hand. Every now and then, I pressed my hands hard around the blanket. I gripped it, tightly, ready for the onslaught of the next wave of pain. It would subside for a second and then resume its wrenching.

'Mum, where are you?'

'You'll get better.' I heard my mother's voice. *'It won't always be like this, Gardenia.'*

'I will, Mum, I will get better.'

I was taken to surgery. I looked at the surgeon who was standing by my side. I knew the anaesthetic had been injected. 'Just do your best,' I said. They were my last words before I fell asleep.

I woke up in a ward and I felt sleepy unable to understand my surroundings. A nurse came up and adjusted a fluid drip and checked other pieces of machinery. I felt a tube or something cold against my thighs. I peered under the bed and noticed plastic tubing. I was hooked up to a bag, a catheter. My first thoughts were of Felixstowe and the time when I couldn't urinate and the possibility of my bladder bursting. *That wasn't my fault, was it? That was because of the medication, wasn't it?*

I fell back into slumber again, tired from the major surgery and the anaesthetic.

I woke again to see the doctors in white coats standing around the foot of my hospital bed.

'We nearly lost you. My assistant surgeon saved your life,' said a tall man wearing a bow tie under his hospital garment. He looked at the younger woman standing next to him. She was short with dark hair and smiled.

'Thank you.' I didn't know what else to say.

After a short interval, the catheter was removed. They wanted me to walk and to move from my bed as soon as possible. The days of recuperating, immobile, in hospital wards had gone. The thought of the toilet and being able to pass fluid made me terrified. I was obsessed with my memory of the catheter and Felixstowe and the hours of agony of having a distended bladder. I didn't want to go through that again.

I went back and forth to the toilet telling myself to relax, this time it will happen. My incapacity to do this basic function made me think I was psychosomatic. *Why am I doing this to myself?*

I took the bedpan and travelled up the elevator to various floors and different toilets. I don't know why I took the bedpan, because after all I was going to a toilet. I wanted to find a nice quiet place and sit in a comfortable position. After many failed attempts, I went back to my ward.

I thought about my countless enemas and purchasing various pharmacy medicines to counteract the excruciating discomfort of constipation. None of them worked – stool softeners, Nulax, Metamucil, Coloxyl. I digested many types of multivitamins and various concoctions, in order to alleviate my anxiety and depression – the vitamin B group, the evening primrose oil, the Remifemin, menopause relief, and liver detox. I was tired of trying to work out ways of excreting matter from my system. It was a continuous battle. *I have to keep going. What else can I do?*

I thought of the CBT and the therapy sessions at Pine View. *Perhaps I have errors in my thinking. Am I catastrophising? Just take some deep breaths. What's the worst thing that can happen? I'll just have another catheter. I'm just seeing things in black and white. I'm being emotional. It's not rational or logical to think I'll never be able to urinate again.*

I went to the ward toilet, my last attempt to relax. I saw a red button on the wall that said press three times in emergency. I felt like my situation was an emergency, so I pressed the button repeatedly. I heard people scurrying and raised voices and then the toilet door opened.

'Oh, you're having a heart attack.' said the nurse sarcastically.

I just looked at her speechless. She shut the door and stormed off.

I went back to my bed and told my nurse that I needed another catheter. 'I can't go. I have been trying for hours,' I said.

She looked at me disapprovingly. 'We can't give you a catheter just because you want one,' she said.

I thought of my extraordinary journey, trying to rationalise human logic and the meaning of insanity. It was a pivotal and enlightening minute of my life. I knew I could think logically. This nurse lacked reasoning and needed to go back to her studies to learn the basics.

'I don't want a catheter because I just feel like it. It's not pleasurable to have plastic tubing stuck in my nether regions.' I tried to explain my predicament. I wanted the nurse to understand my reason for a catheter. 'Do you think I want to retain fluid? If so, then you or I must be really sick and I don't think it's me.'

A doctor arrived shortly after and I was issued with another catheter.

He commented that it was difficult to release urine after having a major operation. I hoped his assurance would help me the next time.

The young woman who was the assistant surgeon paid me a visit. I knew she had saved my life and I realised doctors did have the capability to improve a person's quality of life.

'We found two large tumours in your uterus,' she said. 'One was nineteen centimetres in diameter and the other was thirteen centimetres in diameter.'

One would have been the size of a bowling ball and the other nearly the size of a football.

'They're not cysts but tumours,' the surgeon continued. 'The weight of the tumours changed the gravity in your uterus and this made your fallopian tube strangle your left ovary. It was diseased, so we had to remove this ovary.'

Dead as a doornail.

'I tried to reconstruct your right ovary as I thought you would still like the option of having children. We understand now why you were in such pain. These tumours are called dermoids.'

I could see the front page news: 'Ovaries strangled by fallopian tube.'

'Is it cancer?'

'We don't think so but we'e going to do a biopsy.'

Am I in a Doctor Who episode *and Daleks are about to take over the hospital to avenge the disturbance of their new offspring, their breed of malignant tumours 'the dermoids'?*

'They're common in woman and they're slow growing so they've been in your uterus for some time.'

Well, they wouldn't be common in men.

'What are dermoids?'

'They're full of fibrous tissue like hair follicles. Here, I'll show you the X-ray.'

I followed the surgeon out of the ward to the hallway to see my inner organs through an X-ray light box.

'Here you can see there's a molar. Isn't that amazing?' she said.

I could make out a tooth sitting in the middle of a dark mass.

'A molar? Do you mean a tooth? I have a tooth in a mass of hair, in my uterus?' I was genuinely shocked.

'Yes, it can happen,' said the surgeon.

My first thought was that I wanted to keep the X-ray. It would certainly be a talking point like 'show and tell'. The surgeon refused my request, saying it was needed for further research and study. I acquiesced, knowing improved treatments would mean less pain for others.

Have I been a part of some conspiracy and I've been a test case all these years so they could unearth a mass of hair with teeth from my uterus? I have been watching too many science fiction films. Truth is stranger than fiction and my supposition of having an alien in my stomach has been proved.

I found out later that the tumours were not malignant and I didn't have cancer. After nearly three weeks in hospital, I returned to my own home in Spotswood. I couldn't help thinking that the tumours were the cause of my mental problems but how to prove the connection was another thing entirely. When I questioned the doctor about the cause of such growths, her reply was that she didn't know. I was frequently getting this answer and I wondered if anyone knew anything?

9

My near-death experience was uneventful. I did not see another world or a white curtain and members of deceased persons known to me, waving and welcoming me to a new existence. I did not feel a sense of peace or see a white light. However, the fact that I had nearly succumbed to the grim reaper made me question the cause of the malformed tumours. The worst possible scenario was non-existence and the finality of it made me think that all else was paltry in comparison – except, of course, being locked up in Felixstowe.

My facing possible death was, in a sense, a relief. The weight of my struggles lessened. I had been given a second chance, so to speak. I had faced the worst possible scenario and had beaten the odds. I think the effort of the young surgeon helped me to see the medical system in a new way, although this idea was only superficial. It would need a truck load of apologetic medical staff to appease my pain. My core beliefs were deeply ingrained. My distrust of humanity had permeated my body's cellular structure. How could I loosen the built-up layers of grime, to discard the rotten influence of time?

After the operation, I went home to live with my mother. It was an ironical situation, because she was now looking after me. I still continued to see Doctor Jarvie on a voluntary basis, although having medication meant it was necessary to see her. I was hesitant to stop the chemical cocktails because I did not know what would happen, physically and mentally.

I had made another appointment and was waiting to see her in the hallway that served as the reception area in her rooms at Fitzroy. The large entrance with chairs on one side was the same. It was crowded with seven people waiting their turn. I noticed the menacing face of the apparition. The orange-haired demon had not returned, but the memory of it was not comforting.

I tried to formulate ideas in my mind. Thinking of what I was going to say, how I would approach this next consultation. I tried to use my memory, thinking of recent events, trying to interpret my feelings. This attempt at rehearsal increased my anxiety and I felt like I was on trial again. *I'm a piece on a chessboard and Doctor Jarvie is the player moving me, but is she on my side?*

I wanted to ask the doctor about the tumours. I knew hormones played a big part in mood disorders and controlled emotions. I remembered the time in Felixstowe when my periods were irregular. I didn't want to face another troubling fact that the medication had caused the tumours. It made sense, because the body is finely tuned and ingesting large quantities of chemicals over a long period of time must have an effect.

Are the dermoids the cause of my continued depression and anxiety? I did have an acute anxiety attack at the beginning, related to my abortion. My problems were exacerbated because of the hospital's treatment. My mood swings continued due to dysfunctional hormones. It's all due to being over-medicated, not having a schizoaffective disorder. It's a physical scientific answer, isn't it?

Doctor Jarvie's consulting room was the same. Like an elaborate and comfortable office, with only the desk and piles of papers to differentiate it from a formal lounge area.

'How are you?' said Doctor Jarvie. She was dressed again in a classical outfit. Grey linen trousers and low-heeled shoes to match. Her fawn-coloured blouse had small buds of flowers escaping the cotton surface material.

My physical health has deteriorated. I won't say it's ironical that the health system tried to make me independent but I'm now worse off than before.

'My mother's pleased to see me home, although she is distressed by the fact that I've just undergone a major operation. Which is normal, isn't it.'

Doctor Jarvie nodded. 'I'm very disappointed that the doctors had not picked up on this. With all the physical medical examinations you have undergone.'

Well, it's not much good complaining about it now, is it?

'I have to go back to have a check-up, to have another photograph taken of my uterus. The doctors want to give me a full hysterectomy. They removed the right ovary but they say the left one is diseased.'

I'm twenty-eight years old and I can't have children. Could I have them anyway with the medication?

'Cysts are very common in women,' Doctor Jarvie said.

That explains everything. They aren't cysts, they're tumours. Not fibroids or little lumps on my ovary.

'How are you going at home?'

'My mother's coping well. She's helping me because I'm weak from the operation still. Although I'm tired, I'm able to carry out some basic tasks.' *She does the washing by pressing a button on the machine. I put the clothes on the line. I can't remember what I do at home. Perhaps I should get a dryer.*

'It's a lot for your mother to do, isn't it?'

'She not only loves me but it makes her feel needed and it keeps her independent. Both of us helping each other keeps her out of a nursing home and me out of a mental hospital.'

'Some services are provided. Is that helping you?'

Doctor Jarvie's dark brown eyes looked sad. I wondered if she was about to cry.

'Oh yes, because of my mother's age she's able to access help from the council. The fortnightly cleaning and shopping makes a big difference.'

I wanted to be positive. To say how well everything was going. I didn't want to go back to the halfway house. It was humiliating and patronising to be told how to live, stating the obvious, how to cook, clean and make decisions.

'You do want a place of your own, to be independent?' said the doctor.

Is she making some sort of excuse, blaming me for my circumstances? Thinking I'm not happy, so moving out is the best solution.

'I don't know, perhaps that is the right thing to do,' I said. I needed her help and encouragement. I wasn't sure if I was more afraid of myself or psychiatric hospitals and societies stigma.

'Have you discussed this with your mother? How does she feel about it?'

Is that what Pine View was all about, having me live on my own? She is dogmatic with her approach. She believes in structure, the system's rules and regulations. Pine View is a social conditioning programme and therefore has to be strengthened.

'I've talked with my mother about leaving home. She says you take your mind everywhere you go, you can't escape it by going somewhere different. I mean, you can't get away from yourself.'

'That's very true, but having your own life, that's different. It can make you change your thinking, make you confident and increase your self-esteem. To acknowledge that you're capable. Your mother wants you to be independent. I think that's what she wants for you. To know you'll be okay.'

Is she insinuating my mother is going to die? Everyone is going to die. You have to face life, it's horrid, awful and it will keep on getting worse.

'I can't afford to live away from home. I can't afford to pay the rent and everything else.'

I can't leave my mother. She's been there for me always. She's the only one who has cared. If you understand how sick I've been, not able to understand anything, losing everything, my mind, my memory, then you would understand how important she is to me. She has helped me, so I need her. I can't live without her. I won't survive.

'What are your dreams, Gardenia? What would you really like to do? Where would you like to be in five years' time?'

That's changing the subject. Perhaps she wants to focus on something positive.

'I would like to have written a book on self-help, published a poetry anthology, to have finished my fine arts degree and my bachelor of arts. I would like to have travelled the world at least once and then I would like to be an actress in a comedy series and to sing, with a recording contract.' *I wonder if she'll pick up on my sarcasm.*

'Well, that's a lot,' Doctor Jarvie said.

'Probably a bit too much.'

'Perhaps we'll content ourselves with getting you well first. I think you need to be around people, to participate. I do think you have a lot to offer, Gardenia.'

'I don't have a good memory any more. It's enough for me to remember all my medication. I can't even talk over the phone. I'm scared.'

'What are you frightened of, Gardenia?'

Of you.

'Perhaps we just have to have some happiness enter your life.'

Yeah, and I believe in fairy tales. If only it could be that simple. Their treatment hasn't helped so far.

'I want to eventually come off the medication.'

'That could be possible.'

'The tranquillisers make me sleepy.' I didn't know if it was true, it seemed logical. 'I only take the Alprazolam because it's like a placebo effect. I believe it helps me.'

'Are you still hearing voices?'

'No, they left. They had better things to do.' I didn't know how to answer that question.

'Does that make you feel sad?'

She is trying her best to understand, I suppose.

'No, it was just a phase, a fantasy, a romantic entanglement I had in my head.' *I told her it was because of my not sleeping for eighteen days. She still thinks I'm psychotic.*

'Fantasies play a big part in your life, don't they, Gardenia? You're very creative. Would you like to use your creativity to help others?'

'My fantasies get me into trouble.' *She's a good counsellor, turning my problems into assets.*

'Many people have fantasies. Some find it easier to digest reality with their imagination. It makes life easier.'

'Like religion too.'

'Yes, religion plays a part. It's a comforting thought to many, that there is a God listening to them, understanding their problems.'

'Yeah, but all those people in church, they're not in asylums, are they?'

'In a way, we're all locked in a prison. Everyone wants to be free of their problems. Most of us have to face our dilemmas. Sometimes it's just too hard and we have to seek help.'

'They used to have exorcisms for people like me, didn't they? I'm different and so I'm an evil spirit.'

'Yes, mythologies have played a big part in different cultures. You were telling me you have problems with your memory. Can I ask you to do a test?'

I'm a test case, this is factual evidence. She wants to help, but what else can I do? Tell her to get stuffed and walk out, but say, by the way I need a script.

'Yes, okay, I'll do the test.'

'Can you repeat back to me what I am going to tell you word for word? I'm going to describe a story and I want you to tell the same story back to me. Try to get the words, phrases, everything the same, okay.'

The doctor related a very detailed description of a woman going shopping to the local supermarket. What the woman wore, describing the weather, how she got to the shopping centre. What she bought and the people she met. The checkout operator and what he was wearing and what he said. The list of items she bought. At the end, the woman lost her particular credit card and was unable to pay for the goods. She had to leave the shopping centre and go back home. End of story.

What a frustrating and depressing story. Like the poor woman who lived in a shoe and didn't have anything, even a bone to give to her dog. To be turned away at the last moment because of lack of money. Now the poor woman will starve and probably her dog too. I could see myself in the same situation looking through my handbag, having a panic attack because the other people in the queue were in a hurry. Their watchful eyes regarding me with pity as I frantically fished through my bag.

I related back to the doctor the particular events of the story. I embellished parts because I thought the subject matter was rather dull. I described the people, the woman, her goods, bank accounts and even threw in for good measure additional descriptive details. The kind of shoes customers were wearing. I described the other shops in the vicinity. There was a shoe shop next door, that was having a sale and nearly everyone was there with a long queue of people. Some people were standing in front of the bakery and a new souvenir shop had just opened. I finished by saying the woman had found her credit card outside the door of the shopping centre. She had then gone back to the shops and bought all the goods again. I wanted to point out the merit of persistence and logical thought. I said that the woman did not go hungry and was able to give her poor old dog some dinner.

I watched Doctor Jarvie writing. Her scribble was quick and her handwriting was large. She was going through volumes of paper.

'I'm surprised and amazed that you've repeated nearly every word, perhaps discounting some minor words. The story you've just told me is nearly the exact story I told you. I'm also aware, Gardenia, that you have a very creative mind.'

I smiled. It was the first time a doctor had said anything complimentary about my mental capacity. However, I did not trust her motives. 'You only see sick people in hospital or here in your office, therefore you see only illness. You generalise, but I am an individual. I want to stop taking my medication but I know you're against that.'

'My patients are all individuals in hospital, Gardenia. I've seen enough people in hospital telling me they are fine and go off their tablets. They, of course, relapse.'

'But there must be some who don't.'

'Yes, but they are very few. You see me because you want help. You pay for this service.'

'It's not a case of me wanting to see you. I have to see you, don't I?'

The doctor nodded. 'I understand that you're angry, Gardenia.'

She thinks I'm angry because I have an illness. Like a person would be if diagnosed with cancer and told they were going to die. That I'm unhappy because I've been given a short straw and that life is unfair. She's certainly not going to think the medical system is in the wrong, is she? I wonder how she'd cope if she was told over and over again that her mind was diseased. How much do they really know of the mind? Isn't it a mystery? They still have a long way to go to understand its workings. They don't even know where the mind is.

'I suppose my problems are like a grief process. First of all, I have denial, then anger and then finally acceptance.'

'Yes, I suppose you could say that,' Doctor Jarvie said. Her enthusiasm wasn't encouraging.

'What happens if you're not taking an antipsychotic and you're not psychotic?' I said.

'It means you don't have a psychotic disorder,' she said.

'Do you think I'm psychotic right now?'

'No, I don't think so, but I would advise you to stay on your medication because it prevents you from becoming ill.'

'What caused the tumours?' I thought I would get straight to the point. It was only a forty-minute consultation.

'I'm not sure.'

At least she's honest.

My forty minutes was up. I had to leave the doctor and go home. I caught the bus to Spotswood, relieved to be away from her office, her analysis. My attempts to get support were not gratified. I wanted to forget everything, but this would mean not thinking, stopping all cognition.

I couldn't stop thinking about my illness. I had to live with it daily. The medication reminded me of my fragile mind every morning and night. *She thinks I should just get over it. Perhaps I have bipolar. Would that make me feel better, not to have a psychotic disorder but manic de-*

pression? If I cease the medication, then what will happen? I've put on weight, my sugar levels have increased. I've been diagnosed with diabetes. I have high cholesterol levels. I'm sure the medication has caused this. I will agree with their theories for now.

I wanted to re-enact my consultation with the doctor. I imagined a different conversation.

'I want you to be independent,' said Doctor Jarvie.

'But that's a contradiction in terms, isn't it? I have to take drugs, live in an institution. You just don't trust me,' I said.

'It's a recovery process,' said Doctor Jarvie.

'It's your process and system, not mine. Basically, I'm a test case and you're a warden making sure I don't do anything wrong in society. You're a modern form of Gestapo. I can't be myself, can I? There are conditions. It's not real freedom, is it?'

'Are any of us really free?' Doctor Jarvie replied.

'Some people are, more than others, I think.'

'If you have an illness, then you need treatment,' said Doctor Jarvie.

'I understand treatment orders. Are you threatening me?'

I thought my imaginative conversation was getting out of hand.

My obsessive desire to continually challenge their ideas is making my life hell. If only I could agree with their methods. But their principles are not mine.

I knew that in order to change my situation I would have to play their game. My ceasing medication over time would prove my stability of mind. It was my only arsenal, because they could not discount their own methodology. Their power was science, university degrees, regulations and law. They were an affluent minority, protected. They disguised themselves as healers, but underneath they were diseased and desperate. They were preying on the disadvantaged, the sick and vulnerable and pretending to serve society.

I wondered if I had the courage to face my persecutors. *The biological effects of withdrawal will not be pleasant. Is it just a case of believing in myself.*

The sun's brightness, its light flashing on the bus windows, blinded me. Slowly, its power weakened as it moved further into the lower part of the sky. I sensed that summer was coming to a close and autumn was on its way. The tree branches were moving with the wind and they looked like a chorus of dancers welcoming the new season's arrival, as if it was a rehearsed theme, with choreographic direction. I knew each tree was playing a tune, distinct and different. Patterns like threads of gold glistened on their leaves as the sun made its last attempt to shine, to give them life. I knew it would soon be dark. I wanted it to rain, to hear and see the water gushing along the gutters of the road. To be overcome by nature's sweeping current and to pretend my worries could be swept away.

10

I had decided to retrieve my notes from Felixstowe. It was a necessary undertaking, if I was going to understand my past. The Freedom of Information Act that was passed in Australia in 1991 had allowed me access. This way, I could come to terms with the doctors' ideas, however hard and difficult it would be to relive those times.

I received the documents a month later. My notes were packaged in a yellow post office parcel and I was not surprised by the size: the papers were four inches thick.

I wondered about my intentions and where I would start. I was scared of what the report would reveal, because I knew the contents would be defamatory. It certainly would not be a positive description of my identity or personality.

To understand a theory, a biochemical change in the brain is the subject of a doctoral thesis. Do I have the time or courage to want to study my dilemma?

I felt like I was studying the sea life of the ocean. Human relations, psychological study of a health system and my mind were as mysterious as uncharted waters. The only way I could understand their approach and face the past was to open the files and read the text.

There were pages of documentation and the reports were extensive. Included was a mixture of observation notes taken by nurses. There were doctors' reports and summaries and notes taken while I was being interviewed. There were the neurological examination notes and results. Documentation outlining the numerous blood tests I received and related results. The results of brain scans, EEG, CAT scans and so on. Then there were the outpatient notes covering the seven years I spent sitting in an interview room. The fortnightly visits with student doctors analysing me, questioning my sanity.

I tried to understand the times and dates and to place the events in a logical sequence. My memories came back as I read through the various opinions of doctors. I was horrified to see in writing their ideas and to witness their interpretation of events. Their practical application of psychiatric treatment was barbaric and inappropriate.

I knew I hated myself. I was disgusted by my circumstances, then and now. I was still ashamed of my state, my mind. I expected other people to see me as worthless. When I read the documents and verification of my insanity, I realised the extent of my suffering. Their treatment, their insensitive approach to helping a fellow human being made me feel physically sick. I knew I was not the only one who had mental problems. Their vicious emotional abuse made my 'illness' paltry in comparison. *No wonder I hate myself.*

I read the clinical summary of my hospitalisation. It was written as an overview explaining my illness and behaviour at Felixstowe.

```
History of present illness

Gardenia had her first psychotic episode with her first
admission to open ward. A precipitant to the psychosis was
thought to be an abortion six months previously.
```

Well, that's wrong for a start. I was hospitalised in the first place because they wanted to observe me, to diagnose my complaint. In my first consultation, I was placed on a tranquilliser. I was scared from the outset.

I went back through my notes. Their first idea was that I didn't have a psychotic disorder.

```
No evidence of psychotic thought disorder.
```

It states that in black and white.

I kept on reading their interpretation of my behaviour with their informed opinions. My first hospitalisation was related to having a clinical diagnostic test. Obviously they couldn't find anything wrong with me.

No evidence of thought disorder, but the patient is distressed and confused.

I was suffering an acute anxiety crisis because of the abortion, my circumstances, my anaemia, not eating. Drinking copious amounts of alcohol and taking drugs. They state I was pre-psychotic. What is that when it's at home? Either I was or was not. Did they think I was on the verge? Were they waiting with bated breath for the outcome, hoping it would be so? They wanted me to be ill, but unfortunately they had to state the obvious. There was little evidence of it. I was capable and coherent. Placing me on an antipsychotic medication straight away when there was no evidence of schizophrenia would make anyone question their diagnostic skills.

I remembered my first impressions of Felixstowe hospital. I knew their ideas were wrong. I also knew I didn't have the courage or stamina to tell them I was okay and that I didn't need their services. Because I was unable to understand what was happening to me, they thought it was a sign of psychosis. They saw me as being mentally ill and they just had to prove it. No wonder I felt threatened. I had to prove to them that I didn't have an illness. That I was normal. Their diagnosis was reliant on subjective opinion, nurses' observation. I was scared and I didn't talk. I knew that if I kept quiet, then they couldn't judge me. My withdrawn behaviour was my way of coping. They saw that as a symptom of my illness.

I read their terminology, their description of me 'thought blocking'. They thought because I was not concentrating on anything in particular, I was either hearing voices or having hallucinations. I suppose they didn't consider that their constant questioning, tests and emotional abuse were making me terrified. I wasn't hearing voices or seeing things. I was trying to prove my innocence even then. I understood from the outset that it would be difficult to combat a powerful medical system that wanted to diagnose me with a mental illness.

I continued to read the report.

> Then she was treated in outpatients with some considerable improvement being treated with Imipramine.

That's another lie.

I read back over my notes once again. I had asked for an antidepressant and it was only given to me for a short duration. I expect they thought I was just psychotic.

I continued to read.

> Then again readmitted to open ward, floridly psychotic. Since that time has remained in open ward although with several transfers to secure ward because of absconding behaviour.

That's another lie. I didn't go back to hospital floridly psychotic. I wasn't like that. I was scared because of their treatment. I thought I was going mad because of the side effects. Their tablets were making my life hell, the tremors, falling over, tripping because I couldn't lift my legs. I was unable to function, with the constipation, the dry mouth, the barrage of pimples and acne. I couldn't even sit for more than one minute because of my restlessness. I didn't know if I was coming or going, sedated in mind, yet I couldn't stop moving. How long can a person be like that until something is done? I didn't know of the side effects at that time, that it was the medication doing this to me. I did think it was my fault.

The epileptic fits, the reality tests, their rigorous analyses. Did they encourage or support me? Understand or reaffirm my self-worth or belief? Did they think I would not be emotionally affected by their treatment? It's little wonder I felt persecuted. They thought my fears were paranoid, delusional.

After six months being in Felixstowe, I was allowed to go home but only if my mother took charge of me. If I showed any unusual behaviour, I was to contact Felixstowe.

I tried to return to a healthy lifestyle, participating and socially interacting. I went to pottery classes and art workshops via community support schemes. My endeavours to show them my adequacy was obviously inconsequential.

I left the hospital – 'absconding behaviour' – because I didn't like them or the way they did business. Locking me up was their form of punishment and treatment.

I continued reading the notes.

```
Despite treatment with Imipramine, Fluphenazine and later
Haloperidol and ECT, she has remained psychotic and
depressed.
```

I read the next category or indictment.

```
Mental state examination
```

```
She is a tall, slim red-haired woman who was slow-moving and
cooperative but who wanted to leave the room on several
occasions. There was eye contact but she appeared to be
perplexed. There was very little spontaneous speech and she
spoke in a soft slow voice. She has looseness of association.
Her affect is blunted. She said that she felt down in the
dumps, that she was going to die. And believed that she could
swallow her tongue and there was smoke coming out of her
ears. She was hearing voices in both ears saying 'hello'. She
also heard voices saying that she was dead and that she had to
put her hat on now. She had thought insertion and broadcast
and was receiving messages from the television and radio. She
was fully orientated in person and place but not date. She had
impaired insight and rapport was difficult because of her
blunted affect, thought disorder and perplexity. Physical
examination was normal except for Parkinsonism symptoms and
enlarged pupils, which are side effects of the medication.
```

Had I been hearing things or seeing things that were out of this world, I would have understood. But I was not and their implied assumptions made me feel sick with outrage. I knew why I said those things and I remembered it all. There was a logical explanation.

I was slow-moving with a blunted affect, speaking in a soft, slow voice. Wasn't that due to the medication? Didn't they realise that I was sedated to the eyeballs with enlarged pupils. They didn't say that the medication could make this happen.

They state that I want to leave the room on several occasions. My extreme restlessness and agitation, the side effects of the medication were not taken into account or understood. Maybe I wanted to leave the room because I didn't want to be there or so distressed because of the treatment.

I remembered the sleepwalking, pacing, the dancing in the music room and the choreographic movements in the secure ward. My muscles had seized up.

I continued to read back over previous notes.

```
She still continues to be nervous 'rattling' unable to sit
down for long periods. On edge and is aware of her blood
pulsing. Worse in mornings and she is ultrasensitive.
```

This painful agitation would make anyone lose their interest in life, wouldn't it? I was down in the dumps but that was a logical conclusion on my part. It was amazing and surprising that with all the medication in my system, I could even walk, let alone talk, read or write or remember anything.

They state I had 'looseness of association'. By that time I was probably so confused that it was logical I couldn't form a sentence in my head. That was the basis of their diagnosis, 'my thought disorder'. Did they know that a person loses their short-term memory for six months after ECT?

They state that I believed I was going to swallow my tongue. Did they not see this in relation to my substantial and credible fears of having an epileptic fit? The Parkinsonism affects and the muscle paralysis I was suffering with. Did they understand my fear and perplexity with the ECT? I was strapped down because they didn't have a drug to stop the movement of my limbs, a muscle relaxant. Electroconvulsive therapy was an induced epileptic fit.

My persecutory belief that I was going to die was a very real fear in relation to my circumstances. What I don't understand was their inability to understand. They had little compassion for me. Only theories and textbook jargon.

When I said there was smoke coming out of my ears, I was probably trying to understand recent events. Trying to understand the repeated ECT, my vague understanding of electrocution with electrodes and wires attached to my head. I had three courses of ECT in six months, with three minor operations a week for two weeks. Not one nurse or doctor spoke to me to help me to understand why I was having ECT.

I had to go out and 'put my hat on'. I remembered my mother and I going to town when I was a child and that it was a ritual in which we dressed up. My mother always wore a hat on her head. Did I want to pretend I was going out for the day, to have pleasure, fun? Perhaps I was dreaming of leaving the institution. I didn't want to suffer any more and live without hope in a psychiatric institution.

Why I heard voices in both ears? I know for a fact it was my only way of having any communication at that point. I had to invent someone speaking to me. Someone saying 'hello'. Was that a florid psychotic experience or a woman so traumatised that she couldn't even communicate and had to form some union with something? A voice saying to me that I was dead was probably related to waking up from ECT. I saw other unconscious patients surrounding me and watched nurses continually testing blood pressure. I had undergone an anaesthetic and clinical observations were part of the procedure.

Thought insertion and broadcast was due to my feelings of alienation and confusion. My attempts to fit in were seen as abnormal. Doesn't everyone have this to a degree? Don't we often assume what others are thinking? I ended up believing I was mad.

'Thought broadcasting' means that I believed other people could hear my thoughts. The nurses observed this because I withdrew from conversation. But how could they know, unless I told them?

The recurring message from the television and radio was highly probable, as one does receive ideas and thoughts when they hear other people speak. My lack of cognition with the sedation, the changes in my brain made me frightened and I could not relax and watch the day time soap opera or understand it for that matter. That I repeated my distress to the nurses was seen as yet another symptom of my psychosis.

I did listen to the radio, but did any of the nurses actually stay around long enough to know what I was listening to? If I was listening to a Walkman, then it is highly likely they could not understand what I was hearing. Could they understand my line of thought anyway, unless I told them?

I continued to read the past assault on my mind and body.

Investigations

Complete blood picture normal. CT head scan normal. EEG showed an excess of low voltage fast activity which is non specific or maybe related to medication. The EEG was otherwise in all respects normal.

Thank God for that.

Treatment and progress

Gardenia had a very long admission and evidence of psychosis remained throughout. Initially she appeared quite depressed but this aspect of her mental state seemed to improve with time, until at the time of discharge her affect although labile was most fairly normal.

Eventually lithium was added and she became more obviously affected by the side effects of haloperidol. This was changed to Perphenazine and over the next few months she improved somewhat, although she remained thought disordered with rather grandiose delusions and a few angry outbursts up until the time of her discharge.

My anger outbursts were probably due to emotional exhaustion. My delusions of grandeur were probably due to low self-esteem and self-worth. I wanted to be someone else or somewhere else. Perhaps fantasy was my only hope. That was seen as part of my florid psychosis.

I continued reading the negative prognosis.

```
She was having regular long weekends at home and eventually
came to resist being returned to the ward. Arrangements were
made for her to be discharged into the care of her mother on
the understanding that she can be returned for admission or
for respite for her mother as necessary.
```

```
Medication on discharge
Temazepam at night
Prothiaden at night
Lithium morning and at night
Senokot to relieve constipation
Benztropine morning and night
Lorazepam prn (when requested.)
Perphenazine morning and night and prn
To see doctor regularly in outpatients.
```

I knew my fear of insanity was strongly related to the treatment I received and if I agreed with them, my worries would lessen. I knew I had to agree with their decisions and judgement in order to survive. I told them when and why I needed the medication. At least that way I had some control over my existence. (The prn, taken as required.) The treatment was a social conditioning method, a business agreement. I was pressured to live with their structure or die. My mind had deteriorated to such an extent that I could not fight their plans for me any longer, not whilst in hospital.

I remember just before my discharge, my need for a safe environment. My terror was significant, as I would go to the observation room next to the nurses' station and lie down on the bed. I would say to the nursing staff that I was sorry, if they could please help me. I said over and over to myself, 'I will be all right, I will be all right.' I think they recognised my acceptance of my illness or their treatment of me. I wanted their help.

As an outpatient, I began to work out their methods and what the tablets were for. My repeated frustration, anxiety and anger at not being able to basically function were not understood. I think they saw it as a minor problem in relation to my 'thought disorder'. The hospital experience exacerbated my fears but they saw it as part of my illness, diagnosed with persecutory idealisations.

Then I read about my irregular periods and how this was noted.

She says she is not distressed by this.

Probably I had enough to worry about. Then it dawned on me: irregular periods, why? The tumours in my uterus, why?

I sought to find answers on the internet. A current gynecological study outlined the reason and cause for dermoid tumors in the uterus. I tried to simplify the findings, so I could understand.

Dermoids are caused by increased prolactin in the body. Prolactin is controlled by the neurotransmitters in the brain. Dopamine is a hormone that regulates prolactin. A typical antipsychotic regulates dopamine. Decrease in dopamine inhibitors increases the amount of prolactin.

The results and the implications of this finding gave me hope. It was another significant detail confirming their inappropriate treatment and negligence. My later years with mood swings, anxiety and depression were likely caused by the irregular or malfunctioning hormones. I was overmedicated and therefore susceptible to the occurrence of growths such as tumors.

I knew that irrespective of symptoms or other people's reactions, it was eventually up to me to change my thinking and my life. I couldn't keep on with the anger, reliving this trauma.

I continued to see Doctor Jarvie. The lessening dosages of medication improved my mental alertness and memory and I was less slow-moving. I went back to Kensington Clinic several times, with anxiety and depression. The different environment at the clinic and the comfortable surroundings without a prison-type reality or interrogation helped me to retrieve a measure of trust in human beings.

I had to work on two levels. I had to pacify the doctor's theory while also knowing my own needs, my rights as an individual. It was hard for my doctor not to see me as schizophrenic when my past had said otherwise. My recovery consisted of many variables. First I learnt about my tablets – their properties and their definition. Why I was given them and for what reason. My research on the process of grief helped me to understand my mind and the concept of healing. denial, anger, acceptance, and these three aspects I juggled continually. I was confused with the meaning of reality and how to believe in self when the core of my personality had been demoralised and removed.

I gradually lost my fear of institutions. I used the concepts of CBT. What was the worst thing that could happen? Of course it was Felixstowe, but I knew the strength of my mind and how I managed to beat the odds. I recovered a better quality of life because I did not believe in the health system, their definitions and diagnosis. I used their tools and techniques to overturn their theory. Like post-traumatic stress disorder, I knew I could harness the distressing ideas and stop them reoccurring. I could replace them with positive images and theories.

Challenging my thoughts seemed too simple a task and my problems were far too complex. I tried to become aware of my automatic thinking and was amazed at the numerous negative thoughts that went through my mind. The distortions or assumptions that weren't valid. I tried to understand the pros and cons of my selective thinking. To recognise that my response to certain events and situations was understandable and rational. I wanted simple explanations and was tired of blaming others, the system or myself. I knew that life was more complex than just pulling things apart, understanding feelings, like you would study a specialised subject. Everything was related like a jigsaw puzzle and I knew that some pieces in my life were definitely missing.

The cognitive behavioural therapy was a difficult concept to understand and implement. Although it was a simple idea, in an intellectual sense, it was complex when trying to solve emotional problems. I attempted to change my 'errors in thinking'. It wasn't just a case of what was right or wrong, real or imagined.

To be aware of automatic thoughts was difficult enough, without trying to analyse them. Even so, I liked this therapy, because I could assess my own mind, live my own life. I was in control of my recovery plan. I couldn't change the past or real events and circumstances, but I could control my reaction towards them.

I wanted to prove my sanity and that would mean ceasing the antipsychotics. It was evidence built on scientific means and that was my last vestige of proof. Tranquillisers stop psychosis and not having tranquillisers in the body and not having a psychotic episode meant you didn't have the disorder. I knew the doctors' answer would be that I had recovered and that my illness was in remission. The probability of a good outcome is high if you take the medication for a long period.

I understand why people don't like these hospitals and patients are angry. I think it's a logical conclusion, and a healthy one, to want to get better. To not want to live in an institution, or take medication that destroys the body and soul.

I couldn't withdraw from the tablets overnight. I knew the outcome. My brain had changed to compensate. I couldn't stop taking the medication. I knew the consequences. The agony I would go through.

My abnormality had been drummed into me, it was a core belief in my system, and I had to continually tell myself that I was a worthwhile human being. I was normal and hoped the rest of society would agree.

I will really never know what did happen in Felixstowe. I can only create a new life based on logical assumption, an affirmation that my life is important, not to be discarded, thrown into an institution without release. I had been certified as insane – their definition – but I knew I was not. It was my mission to become an everyday person but what did that mean?

www.ingramcontent.com/pod-product-compliance
Lightning Source LLC
Chambersburg PA
CBHW030910080526
44589CB00010B/227